Dining
in
HISTORIC
TENNESSEE

A Restaurant Guide With Recipes

by Marty Godbey

Illustrations by James Asher

McClanahan
Publishing House

Library of Congress Catalog Card Number: 88 061759
International Standard Book Number: 0-913383-11-2

Cover photograph: Miss Mary Bobo's, Lynchburg, Tennessee

Illustrations by James Asher
Cover photographs by Frank Godbey
Cover design by James Asher
Manufactured in the United States of America

All book order correspondence should be addressed to:
McClanahan Publishing House, Incorporated
P.O. Box 100
Kuttawa, Kentucky 42055
(502) 388-9388

INTRODUCTION

Was it natural beauty, adventure, or the promise of freedom that attracted the first settlers to the west? Like a great green magnet, the over-the-mountain country drew land-hungry people who defied laws and risked Indian attack to settle in its broad valleys.

They fought for the land, colonized it, and pushed ever westward, those first determined few, followed by men rewarded with land for winning an impossible war. Later, people escaping poverty or intolerance in Europe, and those brought here in bondage, made their contributions to a unique culture.

In common, they had confidence in themselves and their abilities, and ambition that would improve their lives and those of their neighbors. They were hunters and farmers and merchants and industrialists— and opportunists— who changed a raw wilderness into homes and jobs and futures.

Differences, engendered in part by geography, were not always easily or kindly solved; Tennesseans fought and died on both sides in a tragic war on her own soil; Native Americans were driven from their homes into alien lands; newcomers were eyed with suspicion.

Despite regrets, there is great pride in Tennessee's rich and diverse history. The distance between Bristol and Memphis is more than a day's drive on the highway; it covers the period from 1750 to the present, from Dr. Thomas Walker to Elvis Presley, and travels three states in one: mountainous East Tennessee, rolling Middle Tennessee, and flat West Tennessee, with people as different as the terrain.

And yet they're all Tennesseeans, open, generous, and hospitable. From the earliest settlers, they've always been eager to share fresh-killed game, corn pone cooked in ashes, spirits made of corn and limestone water— whatever they had.

Tennessee food is more diversified today. Traditional regional favorites are joined by innovative methods of preparation and products new to the area. Ready availability of fresh seafoods has been an important influence, as has an awareness of diet and nutrition in today's restaurant-goers.

A few establishments that provided food and lodging for early

3

Tennesseeans are still in business; many other buildings of historic significance have been restored or refurbished and converted into restaurants. A tavern that sheltered stagecoach travelers after a hard day's journey now serves tourists who cover that distance in less than an hour. Early resorts where city-dwellers "took the waters" or avoided summer heat continue to provide stress-free relaxation, and busy office workers lunch in business structures where their counterparts worked in the past.

Nineteen houses, both elegant and simple, twelve commercial buildings, two schools, and a warehouse have been adapted as restaurants, preserving their unique qualities and offering patrons a little history with their food.

Such unlikely structures as train stations, a church, a fire house, and a castle have been successfully converted to restaurants, giving new visitors an opportunity to observe at first hand some of the places their ancestors took for granted.

These unusual buildings join nine inns and hotels that have provided food and lodging for generations, and continue to do so today.

There are no two alike, and because they belong to people who value the past enough to utilize old buildings, despite the attendant inconveniences, they are all very special places.

A visit to any of Tennessee's restaurants in historic buildings is well repaid, for an awareness of the past is as easily absorbed as the excellent food, and the diner leaves satisfied in more ways than one.

Using DINING IN HISTORIC TENNESSEE
as a Travel Guide

A list of nearly 200 restaurants in historic buildings in Tennessee was accumulated from advertisements, history books, old travel guides, word-of-mouth reports, and personal experience. Each restaurant was investigated, and those selected for *Dining in Historic Tennessee* were chosen on a basis of historic, architectural, and culinary interest (frequently all three) coupled with business stability.

Because Tennessee's tradition of hospitality is carried out so thoroughly in her restaurants, selection was often difficult, and the ultimate decision was made on preservation/restoration grounds. Of the 50 buildings which house the 51 restaurants included, 24 are on the National Register of Historic Places. In addition, those chosen all met the final criterion: they are places a first-time visitor would describe enthusiastically to friends.

The author, often with companions, ate anonymously in every restaurant at least once, ensuring the same treatment any hungry traveler might receive. No restaurant paid to be included or was told of the project until asked to participate. Without exception, restaurant owners and managers have been enthusiastic, gracious, and cooperative, some providing recipes that had never before been disclosed.

As an aid to travelers, restaurants are listed roughly from east to west. Resource information between text and recipes provides addresses and telephone numbers, and all travelers are encouraged to call before driving long distances.

Laws governing the sale of alcoholic beverages vary greatly. If beverages are available, it will be so indicated in the resource information. Most dry areas permit "brown-bagging," or bringing your own, but it would be wise to inquire ahead.

Symbols used for brevity include charge card references: AE= American Express, CB= Carte Blanche, DC= Diner's Club, MC= Master Card, V= Visa.

Most of these restaurants would fall into the "moderate" category of expensiveness; an effort was made to include all price ranges. Using dinner entrée prices as a gauge, dollar signs are used to indicate reasonable ($), moderate ($$), and more expensive ($$$). Luncheon prices are usually significantly lower, and the amount of money spent in any restaurant is increased by the "extras" ordered, i.e., appetizers, drinks, and side orders.

In traditional Southern service, main dishes are frequently accompanied by vegetable(s), salad, and often dessert, and in these cases, the price is counted as an entrée price.

Few of these restaurants would be considered expensive by East or West Coast standards; if cost is a determining factor, however, most restaurants will gladly provide a price range over the telephone.

Visitors are cautioned that although some of the restaurants in *Dining in Historic Tennessee* are well off the beaten track, they may be very popular, and busy seasons are determined by local events that are often unfamiliar to non-residents. To avoid disappointment, **CALL AHEAD FOR RESERVATIONS**.

CONTENTS

State of Tennessee

NED McWHERTER
GOVERNOR

Greetings:

Tennesseans today and throughout our state's history have
cooked and enjoyed eating some of the best food our nation has
to offer. This is a publication that shares Tennessee's varied
menu and historical eating places with everyone.

Tennessee is a state built on a strong family foundation.
Cooking secrets passed down through generations make Tennessee
the home of some of the best "family" recipes in our nation.

But we also have a diverse cuisine ranging from tender catfish
to luscious desserts. And our state is as diverse as our
recipes. From the blues sounds echoing through Beale Street in
Memphis, to country music and the Grand Ole Opry in Nashville,
to the mountain melodies of East Tennessee, our state is rich
in history and heritage.

This publication offers a unique look at our food, our culture
and our people. As you tour Tennessee in the pages of this
book, remember that you are sampling some of the same dishes
that Daniel Boone and Andrew Jackson enjoyed.

Sincerely,

Ned McWherter

TENNESSEE

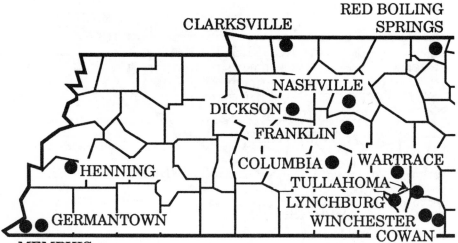

CLARKSVILLE

RED BOILING
SPRINGS

NASHVILLE

DICKSON

FRANKLIN

COLUMBIA

WARTRACE

HENNING

TULLAHOMA

LYNCHBURG

GERMANTOWN

WINCHESTER

COWAN

MEMPHIS

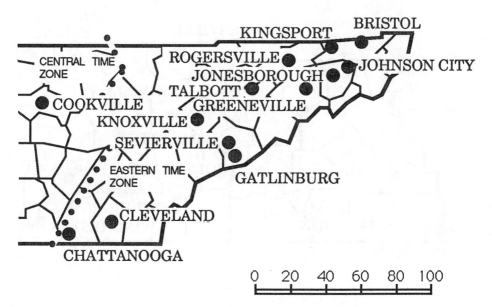

KINGSPORT   BRISTOL

CENTRAL TIME   ROGERSVILLE   JOHNSON CITY
ZONE   JONESBOROUGH
                 TALBOTT
COOKVILLE   GREENEVILLE
KNOXVILLE
SEVIERVILLE
EASTERN TIME
ZONE   GATLINBURG

CLEVELAND

CHATTANOOGA

0   20   40   60   80   100

MILES

THE TROUTDALE
DINING ROOM
Bristol

In the early 1770s, influenced by hunters' tales of rich lands, and believing they were in Virginia, settlers made their homes north and west of the Holston River. Indians protested; these were their lands.

Threatened with Indian attack, the settlers met with three similar groups in 1772 to form the Watauga Association, probably the first attempt at self-government in America. This organization, providing mutual protection from Indians and just enough government to quell lawlessness, was the very beginning of the state of Tennessee.

Captain Evan Shelby's fort at Sapling Grove, later "King's Meadows," was re-named "Bristol" when a town was laid out in 1852.

Charles Robertson Vance, a Bristol lawyer, requisitioned guns for the Confederate Army during the War Between the States. After the war, he took his family to safety in an area of fewer Unionists, returning to his home in Bristol when he was pardoned by President Andrew Johnson.

In the 1890s, Bristol boomed, with land companies promoting growth and at least five railroads servicing the town. An elaborate hotel, a Union railroad depot, and new industries and residences were constructed.

At this time, the Vance home was remodeled into an imposing Queen Anne frame house with a spreading porch. The original structure was more than doubled by an addition on the right side; the roof was raised to a steep pitch, and crested with ornamental iron. The house remained in the family until 1987, when it was purchased to become a restaurant.

Barry and Carol Serber, New Yorkers with a "back to the land" urge, relocated to Southwestern Virginia in the early 1970s, subsequently opening a warm-weather restaurant in a tiny, remote town. The Troutdale Dining Room was successful, but Carol's superb cooking deserved a full-time restaurant, and in 1986, it closed, while the Serbers looked for a more accessible location.

The Vance home in Bristol was perfect, and after painstaking restoration, the Troutdale Dining Room reopened there in June of 1988. Dining rooms are spacious and white, with pastel curtains and matching tablecloths. Original oak woodwork has

15

been skillfully restored; a corner bay window and four tile fireplaces, fitted with gas logs, evoke the Victorian era.

The Serbers' exposure to diverse ethnic cuisines in New York, plus Carol's two years in Mexico, have resulted in a menu of classic dishes from all over the world, interpreted in Carol's style, and individually prepared. Only the highest quality ingredients are used; some are shipped from New York, fresh herbs are locally grown, and trout are swimming in the former creamery behind the house minutes before they are prepared.

"We do fun, international things people can relate to," Barry said, "but different from the way they've had it before."

Think of scallops and shrimp in homemade ravioli, or a trout fillet, stuffed with trout mousse, wrapped in bok choy and served with two bright-colored sauces. Or boned quail, stuffed with mushrooms and wild rice and braised in a wine sauce. Or the hallmark poached trout "Chinese style," enmeshed in strips of scallion and julienne ginger....

Homemade breads and desserts receive the same attention— the ultimate indulgence is Espresso Ice Cream with Kahlúa Chocolate Sauce, or a delicate, creamy Orange Flan in a pool of its own caramel.

The Troutdale Dining Room, 412 6th Avenue, Bristol, is open for dinner from 5 to 9:30 p.m., Monday through Saturday, with café hours (appetizers, desserts, coffees) 3:30 to 11 p.m. (615)698-9099. Dress is casual, all beverages are served, and reservations are preferred. MC, V. ($$$)

TROUTDALE DINING ROOM CEVICHE

1 pound firm-fleshed white fish (halibut, orange roughy, etc.)
Juice of about 8 fresh limes
4 tomatoes, skinned, in 1/2" dice
1 large onion, very finely diced

1/4 cup fresh minced coriander, or to taste
Salt and pepper
1 Tablespoon fresh oregano leaves, chopped, OR
1 1/2 teaspoons dried oregano
3 avacados, halved

2 to 3 cloves garlic,
minced
1/2 cup thinly sliced
Spanish olives
(optional)

1/2 jalapeño or serrano
pepper, very finely
minced

Cut fish into 3/4" cubes; place in stainless or glass pan and marinate in lime juice to cover. Refrigerate 6 hours to overnight; fish will be opaque when done. Drain lime juice, and add remaining ingredients, mixing carefully. Refrigerate until ready to serve. Serve in avacado halves. Serves 6.

TROUTDALE DINING ROOM SHRIMP FRANÇAIS

For 2 servings:
6 Tablespoons sweet
butter, divided
14 extra-jumbo shrimp
(about 1 pound)
1/2 green pepper, in
julienne
1/2 sweet red pepper, in
julienne

3 Tablespoons minced
shallots
Juice of 1/2 lemon
Salt and fresh-ground
black pepper
2-3 scallions, including
green, slivered into 2
or 3" pieces
3/8 cup Noilly Prat dry
vermouth

In sauté pan, melt 3 Tablespoons butter until it sizzles. Add shrimp, sauté 1 1/2 minutes, add peppers and shallots, and turn shrimp; it should be bright pink. Sauté another minute. Squeeze lemon over pan, season to taste, and add remaining butter. When it melts, add slivered scallions and flame with vermouth. Scrape bottom of pan to include dried juices, and serve over a buttery risotto.

WILLIAMSBURG TEA ROOM
Johnson City

In 1854, Henry Johnson, realizing the potential of the railroads, bought, for $50., half an acre at the junction of the proposed railroad and the stage road (now Market Street) in what was then called Blue Plum. He built a store and waited for the East Tennessee and Virginia Railroad, which arrived from Bristol in 1857, and from Knoxville the following year.

At his own expense, Johnson constructed a depot, and when trains stopped, the name changed to Johnson's Tank, then Johnson's Depot; during the War Between the States, it changed to Haynesville, for Landon C. Haynes, a Confederate Senator and resident. When the town was incorporated in 1869, Johnson, by then postmaster, depot agent, shopkeeper, and innkeeper, was unanimously elected first mayor of the town re-named for him.

A boom came to Johnson City in the 1880s. Eastern capitalists invested in a land company, and built a hotel, a blast furnace and a union depot to serve three railroads. Between 1880 and 1890, population increased from 685 to 4,645.

The Campbell Addition, with comfortable houses on wide shady streets, was Johnson City's first residential development. A grocer named Jackson built houses for his children near his own; that of his son was a Colonial Revival cottage with a gambrel roof.

Occupied by a succession of families, the little brick house was first used for business in the early 1980s, when the porch was removed and the interior remodeled. It had been an interior decorator's studio and a florist's shop, when Billie Galloway, a bookkeeper eager to fulfill a long-time dream, purchased it, and in 1985, it became the Williamsburg Tea Room.

The downstairs is pleasantly open, with columns dividing the hall from two cozy dining rooms. Here, and in the seasonal courtyard, what one visitor described as "hearty party food" is served: Jambalaya, with chunks of chicken breast, shrimp, and sausage in a Creole broth, or hot shredded chicken salad casserole, with toasted almonds and cheddar cheese.

Sandwiches range from roast beef on a hard roll to the vegetarian Tea Garden, of Swiss and cheddar cheese, sprouts, cucumber and almonds on whole wheat bread; chicken salad with toasted almonds on a croissant is always popular.

"My favorite part is preparing food and watching people enjoy what I cook," Billie Galloway said, and she's never disappointed in the reaction to her desserts. Whether they choose Coconut Sour Cream Torte, Fresh Apple Cake with ice cream, Lemon Curd Tarts, or the outrageous Chocolate Raspberry Truffle Cheesecake, visitors are thrilled.

And, in keeping with a tea room, they can come back late in the day for more desserts, a pot of tea or coffee, and homemade scones or muffins dripping in honey butter.

The Williamsburg Tea Room, 105 West Holston Avenue, Johnson City, is open for lunch Monday through Friday, 11:30 a.m. to 2:30 p.m. Dinner hours vary; please call. (615)926-7426. Dress is casual, and reservations are accepted, although not necessary, but are required for parties of six or more. Busiest time is December; tea room is closed the first two weeks in January. MC, V. ($$)

WILLIAMSBURG TEA ROOM
CREAMY TOMATO SOUP

1/4 cup minced onion
3 Tablespoons butter
3 Tablespoons flour
3/4 teaspoon salt
1/4 teaspoon pepper

1 cup milk
4 cups tomato juice
1 small bay leaf
Minced parsley for
** garnish**

Sauté onion in butter until tender. Add flour and seasonings, stir until smooth, and cook 1 minute. Gradually add milk and tomato juice. Cook until thick and bubbly, add bay leaf, and simmer 1 minute. Remove bay leaf. Garnish with parsley. Serves 6.

WILLIAMSBURG TEA ROOM
POPPY SEED MUFFINS

3 cups flour
2 1/4 cups sugar

1 1/2 cups milk
3 eggs

1 1/2 teaspoons baking
 powder
1 1/2 teaspoons salt
1 1/2 cups vegetable oil

1/2 teaspoon almond
 extract
1 1/2 Tablespoons poppy
 seeds

In large bowl, combine dry ingredients; in another, whisk oil, milk, eggs, and extract until smooth. Add dry ingredients and stir only until evenly moistened. Stir in poppy seeds. Spoon batter into greased muffin pans and bake at 350 degrees about 30 minutes or until golden brown. Yields 24.

WILLIAMSBURG TEA ROOM
WALNUT FUDGE CAKE

1 1/2 sticks butter
2 teaspoons vanilla
1 1/2 cups sugar
3 egg yolks
3 ounces unsweetened
 chocolate, melted
3 Tablespoons hot water

1/2 cup flour, sifted
3/4 cup coarsely
 chopped walnuts
3 egg whites
Pinch of salt
Pinch of cream of tartar
Chantilly cream
 (below)

Have butter and eggs at room temperature. Cream butter until fluffy, mix in vanilla, and add sugar gradually, beating until fluffy. Add egg yolks 1 at a time, then chocolate and hot water. Stir in flour until smooth, and add walnuts. In another bowl, beat egg whites with salt and cream of tartar until stiff but not dry. Fold into chocolate mixture very gently. Pour batter into greased 9-inch springform pan and bake 1 hour at 350 degrees. Top with Chantilly cream. Serves 8.

For Chantilly cream: Beat together until stiff: 2 cups whipping cream, 2 Tablespoons sour cream, 4 Tablespoons powdered sugar, 2 teaspoons vanilla, and 4 teaspoons cherry brandy (Kirsch preferred).

FIREHOUSE RESTAURANT
Johnson City

When houses were made almost entirely of wood, and the only heat and light came from open flames, the danger of fire was always present, and always dreaded. The earliest method of firefighting was simply throwing water on the fire from buckets or other containers, ineffective at best, and often futile.

The first American fire companies were volunteers: in settlements, residents formed bucket brigades, passing full buckets hand to hand from pond or well to the fire, then returning empty ones to the source.

Ancient Romans had devices for squirting water on fires, but these developed very slowly, with hand-operated pumps in use until well into the nineteenth century. Wooden engines, placed too near fires before hoses came into use, were nearly always burned, and they lacked sufficient power to direct an effective stream. The first mechanical engines were steam powered, drawn by men and/or horses, and were very heavy and cumbersome.

Motor-propelled fire engines came into being about 1903; Johnson City's first was a 1913 American LaFrance, when firemen shared quarters with policemen and the city jail. A bond issue provided funds for the first two fire stations: Headquarters Station, built in 1929 on East Watauga and still in operation, and #2 Station, built in 1930 on West Walnut.

The brick bungalow looked much like houses of the period, except for the garage doors— the engine was housed downstairs, and Chief L.L. Geisler lived upstairs.

When Tom Seaton and his partner outgrew their carry-out barbecue business, they purchased the #2 Station from the city and opened it as a restaurant in January, 1981. Tom, a great-nephew of former Johnson City Fire Chief Ed Seaton, began searching for Fire Department pictures and artifacts with which to decorate the restaurant. Axes, hoses, hats and the station's original plaque make interesting conversation-starters, and the 1928 Seagraves fire engine out front adds to the atmosphere.

The main dining room, in the garage portion, has a raised section, with brass rails; a second dining room is in the former bunkroom. The Chief's apartment upstairs is for overflow and private parties.

With Tom as sole owner, the Firehouse Restaurant now serves three meals a day, with barbecue accounting for only 30 per cent of the business. It is, however, excellent barbecue, tender, delicately smoked meat, with no gristle or fat, flavored by two entirely different but equally good sauces. All barbecue is smoked on the premises over hickory logs, as are other smoked meats, including about 400 smoked turkeys at Christmas.

"We have two old brick pits fired with nothing but wood," Tom said. "It's a little bit more trouble, a little bit more expense, but well worth it for the flavor."

He's willing to go the extra mile for other foods, as well. Scratch buttermilk biscuits with "Sawmill" gravy (ground sausage in milk gravy) are crowd pleasers at breakfast, which also offers a choice of eight varieties of pancakes (including chocolate chip, peach, etc.), big puffy blueberry muffins, and a four-ounce rib eye with eggs and hashbrowns. There are superb cinnamon fried apples on weekends.

Sandwiches reflect the smoked meats people have come to expect: club sandwiches have smoked ham and smoked turkey, and you can create your own deli combinations of smoked meats and cheeses. Dinner specials vary, but might be Steak and Shrimp— a rib eye with char-broiled barbecued shrimp, basted with the Firehouse sweet sauce.

Topping it off are homemade desserts such as Chocolate Delight, a gooey, chewy chocolate chip pie served in a deep glass bowl with ice cream; cheesecake; strawberry pie; and Apple Pan Dowdy, an upside down apple cake, with spiced apples and cinnamon, topped with ice cream and caramel.

The Firehouse Restaurant, 627 West Walnut, Johnson City, is open for breakfast every day: 6:30 to 10:30 a.m. Monday through Friday, until 11:30 a.m. Saturday, and 8 to 11:30 a.m. Sunday. There is continuous service for lunch and dinner until 9:30 p.m. weekdays and Sunday, until 10 p.m. Friday and Saturday; dinner specials begin at 5:30 p.m. (615)929-7377. Dress is casual, all beverages are served, and reservations are accepted, but not required. AE, MC, V. ($)

FIREHOUSE RESTAURANT UNCLE HARRY'S
SMOKED TURKEY SALAD

1 cup mayonnaise
1/4 cup Durkee's
 Sandwich Sauce
1/4 Tablespoon coarsely
 ground pepper
Juice of one lemon
 wedge

1 1/2 pounds smoked
 turkey, in small
 chunks
1/4 cup chopped celery
1/2 cup dill pickle cubes

In mixing bowl, combine first 4 ingredients thoroughly. Add smoked turkey, blend well, then add celery and pickle and blend. Serve on sandwiches or as a salad.

Tom Seaton encourages home barbecue cooks to try smoking their own turkey for this recipe, although smoked turkey is available at most delicatessens.

FIREHOUSE RESTAURANT
CHOCOLATE DELIGHT

One 10-inch unbaked pie
 shell
1 cup flour
2/3 cup sugar
2/3 cup chopped pecans
1/2 cup oatmeal

2 eggs
1/4 cup melted butter
1/4 teaspoon vanilla
2/3 cup semi-sweet
 chocolate chips

Prepare pie shell. In mixing bowl, combine next 4 ingredients. In another bowl, blend eggs with butter and vanilla, then add to flour mixture. Fold in chocolate chips and pour into pie shell. Bake 20 minutes at 325 degrees in convection oven, longer in conventional oven. Serve warm with vanilla ice cream.

THE BLUE IRIS TEA ROOM
Jonesborough

In 1779, Tennessee's first town was established as the seat of Washington County, North Carolina; in the seventeen years before Tennessee became a state, Jonesborough also served as the first capital of the short-lived State of Franklin.

After the Revolution, the impoverished United States suggested the states cede their western lands to the nation to resolve border disputes and replenish the national treasury. Many states did so, and in 1784, feeling abandoned by North Carolina, representatives from East Tennessee's three counties met at Jonesborough to declare independence.

The Free State of Franklin adopted a constitution patterned after that of North Carolina, and John Sevier was elected governor. Neither North Carolina nor the United States recognized the new state, however, and for a time there were two rival governments in the area. With the expiration of Sevier's term in 1788, Franklin came to an end, but its leaders were important in establishing the new state of Tennessee.

In 1858, on "Rocky Hill" overlooking Jonesborough and adjoining the town's old cemetery, Holston Baptist Female Institute was opened in a spacious, two story, red brick house with wide porches. The school provided primary and secondary education to girls from Jonesborough and the surrounding area.

Unsafe travel during the War Between the States forced the school to close after only three years, and the building served as a hospital for both Union and Confederate wounded during the conflict. Following the war, it was used as a boys' school, a Quaker school for Blacks, and a private residence. As part of the Jonesborough Historic District, it was placed on the National Register in 1969.

In the early 1980s, the house was returned to its former elegance and adapted into apartments, but by the summer of 1984, two of those apartments had become a restaurant and an art gallery. The Blue Iris Tea Room, named for the State Flower of Tennessee, occupies the first floor, where high ceilings and two-tone blue woodwork set off antique tables adorned with blue mats and blue and white flowers.

The tea room is operated by Beth Musser and Charles Caudle, who "try to provide the highest quality food with an eye to presentation and detail," Charles said. Their innovative approach to luncheon provides more than fifty different specialties. "Unless we were requested to do so," Beth said, "we probably wouldn't serve the same thing more than three times a year."

Frequent requests have resulted in a menu that features House Favorites such as the Louisiana Bay Shrimp Sandwich, individually prepared Salad Entrées, and hearty sandwiches. And the House Entrée might have Greek, Italian, or American origins, while emphasizing seasonal fruits and vegetables.

The Blue Iris signature dessert is Glacé Suisse: vanilla ice cream, rolled in toasted coconut and toasted almonds, served in a Margarita glass with their own Swiss Chocolate Sauce and gobs of whipped cream.

The Blue Iris Tea Room, 233 East Main Street, Jonesborough, is open for luncheon only, 11:30 a.m. to 2:30 p.m. Tuesday through Saturday, and on Summer Sundays from 11:30 to 2 p.m. (615)753-5100. Dress is casual, and reservations are accepted, and preferred for parties of 6 or more or when a private dining room is requested. Reservations are a necessity during the Storytelling Festival, the first full weekend each October. No credit cards are accepted, but personal checks are. ($$)

BLUE IRIS SPINACH AND FETA FEUILLETÉE

8 ounces cream cheese, softened
10 ounces crumbled feta cheese
Two 10-ounce packages frozen chopped spinach, thawed, drained, and squeezed dry
2 eggs
1 1/2 teaspoons lemon pepper
1/4 cup sliced black olives (optional)
Two 10" x 15" sheets puff pastry dough
1 egg, beaten with 1 Tablespoon cold water

In large bowl, combine first 6 ingredients. Place 1 sheet of thawed pastry on baking tray, brush edges with egg/water mixture, then spread filling evenly to within 1/2 inch of edge.

Sprinkle with optional olives. Place second sheet of pastry on top, pressing edges to seal to first sheet. Brush top with egg wash. With SHARP knife, score top into bite-size squares for appetizer servings or larger squares for luncheon servings. Prick pastry with fork 12 times to vent. Bake on center rack in preheated 400 degree oven 20-25 minutes, or until well browned. Cool on rack 10-15 minutes, then cut with SHARP knife. Serve warm or at room temperature.

BLUE IRIS HONEY-GINGER GLAZED CARROTS

4 Tablespoons unsalted
  butter
2 teaspoons grated fresh
  ginger OR
1 teaspoon dry ginger
Salt and pepper

1/2 cup water
6 to 8 medium carrots,
  peeled and sliced
2-3 Tablespoons clover
  honey

In 10" skillet, melt butter, and add next 4 ingredients. Cover tightly and steam 5 to 6 minutes. Remove lid, and cook until most of the water is evaporated. Add honey and stir to coat evenly. Serves 4 to 6.

BLUE IRIS SWEET AND SOUR SALAD DRESSING

1 1/4 cups cider vinegar
3/4 cup salad oil
1 teaspoon salt
1 1/2 cups sugar

1/4 teaspoon paprika
2 generous teaspoons
  pressed fresh garlic

Combine all ingredients in quart jar with tight-fitting lid. Leave at room temperature for several hours, shaking occasionally to dissolve sugar. Dressing will keep several weeks in refrigerator; it is particularly good on a fresh spinach salad.

THE PARSON'S TABLE
Jonesborough

Within ten years of the first permanent white settlements in East Tennessee, churches were established in most little towns and in some remote areas as well. Few, however, had a full-time minister. When the traveling preacher came, families of all faiths gathered, weddings and baptisms were held, and those who lived too far away to return home between services camped on the ground.

Around 1800, growing out of "camp meetings," a widespread religious fervor swept the frontier. Thousands of people attended outdoor revivals, and many of them, overpowered by emotion, were seized with involuntary spasms called "the jerks." Any preacher who could interpret the Gospel in the independent spirit of the Frontier found followers; within denominations unable to adapt were divisions.

The Presbyterian church, in which individual churches belonged to a parent organization, lost ground to Methodists and Baptists, who could establish independent churches and did not require an educated clergy. The Cumberland Presbyterians pulled away from their established church in 1809, following the Christian Church, which, in 1804, had hoped to bring all denominations together, but succeeded in forming a new one. Baptists split into dozens of dissenting groups divided by such points as foreign missions and eternal damnation.

The "Great Revival" ended about 1810, having affected not only religion, but politics and education for all time.

During the War Between the States, Unionist members of the Jonesborough Presbyterian Church broke away from their parent church, and built another.

About 1873, when the First Christian Church was under construction, a cholera epidemic swept the state, and all but ninety of Jonesborough's citizens fled. Of these, forty died, including the church's primary financial backer. Despite these setbacks, the congregation grew, and when the Presbyterians reunited in the twentieth century, the Christian Church moved into their second building for larger quarters.

The lovely little Gothic Revival structure which had been their home was deconsecrated, and has served as a temperance hall, lecture hall, woodworking shop, and a restaurant. Originally built with the floor above a crawl space, the building was altered in the 1950s by the lowering of that floor to ground level; otherwise, it is much the same.

Jeff and Debra Myron, a husband and wife team, took over The Parson's Table in September of 1986, and redecorated to emphasize the building's Victorian aspects. Black-background floral wallpaper is set off by white painted woodwork and balcony railing, and tables with raspberry-colored cloths are fitted out with oil lamps, spoon holders, and other accouterments of the period, both in the church and the adjoining former parsonage.

Victorian charm extends even to apparel: Debra, as hostess, wears a high-necked gown with leg-of-lamb sleeves, waitresses are in long, black dresses with white caps and aprons, and waiters wear black trousers and waistcoats, their flowing sleeves retained by sleeve garters.

This same attention to detail is reflected in the food, which Chef Jeff described as "Continental dining with a heavenly touch," executed for "conservative people with sophisticated tastes."

The luncheon menu offers classic appetizers, and includes casseroles, crêpes, and entrées such as Cranberry Chicken, as well as hearty sandwiches and entrée salads. Hot honey-wheat bread begins an evening meal that might feature Rack of Lamb Dijonnaise or hand-cut Burgundy Rib Eye, marinated in wine and seasonings. Salads are crisp, with homemade dressings, vegetables are al dente, and well-named "Sinful Conclusions" begin with homemade ice creams and go on to Strawberry Amaretto Cake, Bavarian creams, and rich Williamsburg Pecan Pie.

And on the seventh day, there's a bountiful brunch buffet for a sampling of all your favorites.

The Parsons Table is on a hill a block off Main Street, behind the Washington County Courthouse in Jonesborough. (615)753-8002. It is open for lunch 11:30 a.m. to 2 p.m., Tuesday through Sunday, and for dinner Tuesday through Saturday, 5:30 p.m. until the seating of the last reservation. Dress is casual, although most men wear jackets, and reservations are appreciated, and are necessary Friday and Saturday and during Historic Jonesborough Days in July, and the National Storytelling Festival the first full weekend in October. MC, V, personal checks. ($$).

PARSON'S TABLE KIWI CUSTARD ICE CREAM

5 kiwi, peeled and diced
1 cup sugar, divided
One 14-ounce can
  sweetened condensed
  milk

4 egg yolks
Dash of salt
1 Tablespoon vanilla
2 cups heavy cream

Mix kiwi with 1/2 cup sugar; refrigerate 2-3 hours. In double boiler, blend yolks with remaining sugar, condensed milk, and seasonings. Stir and cook over simmering water about 10 minutes. Remove from heat and add cream and kiwi. Place mixture in ice cream freezer and freeze according to manufacturer's instructions.

PARSON'S TABLE WILLIAMSBURG PECAN PIE

One 8-inch unbaked pie
  crust
1 cup pecan halves
4 eggs
3/4 cup sugar
1/2 teaspoon salt

1 1/2 cups light Karo
  syrup
1 Tablespoon melted
  butter
1 teaspoon vanilla

Preheat oven to 400 degrees. Place pecans in crust. Mix remaining ingredients without incorporating air. Pour filling over pecans, place pie in oven, and reduce temperature to 350 degrees. Bake 40 to 50 minutes, until evenly browned. Cool before serving.

KINGSPORT GROCERY CO.
Kingsport

The Long Island of the Holston River, nearly four miles in length, was a landmark to Indians; a fording place nearby was part of a Cherokee trail. Discovered by Dr. Thomas Walker in 1750, the trail was used by Daniel Boone as part of the Wilderness Road.

A series of forts was established beside the trail, and boats transporting materials down the Holston and Tennessee rivers landed here. In 1774, Colonel James King built a large stone mill at the mouth of Reedy Creek on the south fork of the Holston, and later constructed a tavern and an ironworks.

The Cherokee, angered by encroachment on their lands, sided with the British during the Revolution and were defeated in the battle of Island Flats in 1776, considered the first Revolutionary battle west of the Alleghenies. On July 20, 1777, they met with representatives from Virginia and North Carolina to sign the Treaty of the Long Island of the Holston. By this document, Indians gave up certain lands and created a boundary not to be crossed by any white man "on any pretense whatsoever," a promise that was not kept.

Early nineteenth century development in Kingsport included the building of four powder mills, an iron works, and various mills, but as the Holston became unnavigable and railroads favored other towns, Kingsport declined. When the Carolina, Clinchfield, and Ohio Railroad came through in 1909, an improvement association decided to establish a planned industrial city on the old Indian battle site: a Model City.

On Main Street, near the railroad station, manufactories, and other wholesale businesses, the Kingsport Grocery Company opened in 1916. The plain-fronted three story red brick structure housed offices and stores of wholesale grocery supplies and hardware. It remained under the same management until it was purchased in 1985, and remodeled into a restaurant.

Retaining its original name, the Kingsport Grocery Co. also keeps many of its features. It is open and airy, with high ceilings and old woodwork, and interesting nooks and crannies have been created for tables of various sizes.

It's the kind of restaurant where people of all ages feel comfortable, munching on cheese fingers or "Chicken Lips" and inspecting a menu that includes salads, sandwiches, burgers with quaint names (such as "The Lind," "The Hinden," "The Duesen," etc.) and some interesting entrées. Charbroiled shrimp in a lemon wine sauce, for instance, or blackened strips of prime rib sautéed with peppers, onions, and tomatoes. Chicken Monterey, a marinated filet with peppers, onions, mushrooms, and jack cheese, was invented here, and remains popular.

Two desserts are musts: the sinfully rich chocolate Fudge Pie, and Jimmie Lee Pie, a thick, fat chocolate chip cookie in a crock, served hot with ice cream and hot fudge sauce.

The Kingsport Grocery Co., 453 East Main Street, Kingsport, is open 11 a.m. to 5 p.m., Monday through Saturday, and for dinner 5 to 10 p.m. Monday through Thursday, until 11 Friday and Saturday. (615)378-3800. Dress is casual, all beverages are served, and reservations are accepted, requested for parties of five or more. Busiest time is during Fun Fest, in early August. AE, MC, V. ($$)

KINGSPORT GROCERY CO. CHICKEN STIR FRY

For each serving:

1 Tablespoon oil
6 ounces chicken, cubed
7 snow peas
1/2 cup pineapple
   chunks
2 ounces diced, blanched
   onion

2 ounces chopped, diced
   red and green peppers
1/4 tomato, in 4 wedges
4 ounces sweet and sour
   sauce
4 ounces rice pilaf,
   cooked

Heat oil in wok. Add chicken and stir fry until chicken turns white. Add snow peas and cook until heated through. Add pineapple, onion, peppers, and tomato, and heat thoroughly. Add sweet and sour sauce, bring to a boil, and serve over rice.

KINGSPORT GROCERY CO. CHEESE AND MUSHROOM SOUP

1 1/4 pounds mushrooms,
   sliced
2 sticks margarine

2 teaspoons Tabasco
8 ounces shredded
   cheddar cheese

2 cups flour
2 quarts strong chicken
   stock

2 cups heavy cream
2 cups warm milk

In saucepan, cook mushrooms in a little water until tender. Set aside. In large pot, melt margarine and whisk in flour until smooth. Whisk in chicken stock and Tabasco, then stir in cheese, cream and milk. Stir over low heat until creamy; add mushrooms. Serves 10.

KINGSPORT GROCERY CO. INDIVIDUAL DEEP DISH APPLE COBBLER

Pie dough for 1 pie
1 cup sugar
1/2 cup dark brown
   sugar
1 teaspoon cornstarch
1 teaspoon cinnamon
1/4 teaspoon nutmeg

1/2 teaspoon grated
   lemon rind
2 Tablespoons brandy
2 pounds sliced apples
   (fresh or canned,
   drained)
Cinnamon sugar (below)

Roll out pie dough and cut into 4 circles, about 6" each. Set aside. In bowl, mix dry ingredients. Place apples in large bowl, sprinkle with brandy, then add sugar mixture and toss to coat apples evenly. Divide mixture into 4 onion soup bowls, top with crust, and flute edges. Slash each crust 4 times; sprinkle with cinnamon sugar and bake 10 to 15 minutes at 425 degrees. To serve, press scoop of ice cream in center of each pie, breaking crust slightly. Serves 4.

For Cinnamon sugar: mix 1/2 cup sugar with 1 teaspoon cinnamon; store in shaker. Use extra for cinnamon toast.

DOAK HOUSE
Greeneville

The defiant Scotch-Irish settlers who came into the Over-the-Mountain country were sustained by fierce independence and a sense of equality that grew out of their religious backgrounds. Although most were originally Presbyterian, that doctrine's emphasis on education for its ministers created a shortage on the frontier, and many settlers were drawn to fiery Methodist and Baptist preachers.

Several of Tennessee's early religious leaders established schools that became the foundation of the state's first colleges and universities. The earliest of these was begun by Samuel Doak, a Presbyterian from Virginia, who crossed the mountains on foot about 1779, his horse bearing the first books to come into the area. On Little Limestone Creek, near Jonesborough, he founded Salem Presbyterian Church and Martin Academy, which became Washington College in 1795.

In 1818, leaving those institutions in the hands of his oldest son, Doak moved fifteen miles west and founded Tusculum Academy with his second son, Samuel W. Doak. Tusculum College, an outgrowth of that school, is the oldest college in Tennessee.

The brick structure built by the Doaks housed the school initially, and was home for both educators until their deaths. It remained in the Doak family until 1974. Now the property of Tusculum College, it was restored by the Greene County Heritage Trust, and was placed on the National Register in 1975.

A dignified two-story house of Georgian design, constructed of brick laid in Flemish bond, The Doak House faces Frank's Creek across a shaded lawn, its rear elevation toward the road. The house has been changed very little over the years; modern plumbing, electricity, and gas were installed for the first time when it became a restaurant in 1986.

The living room, cozy with a quilt-draped settle before the fire, features an enormous original sideboard made to match the house's eight mantels. Here, and in the dining rooms, where painted woodwork brightens whitewashed walls, tall windows with their original panes overlook the peaceful countryside. Upstairs, shops in former bedrooms provide additional viewing.

Jack Whalen, a Michigan native who has been in the restaurant business since 1970, operates the restaurant to create "a quiet, secluded kind of atmosphere." He offers American food that changes with the seasons, and reflects the interests— and often the recipes— of his customers.

There's a different lunch special every day: fried chicken on Tuesday, baked ham and potato salad on Wednesday, etc., added to a Crêpe of the Day, soups, salads and sandwiches.

At dinner, an expanded list of appetizers includes tasty crabmeat stuffed mushrooms, and hearty dinner salads join beef, veal, poultry, and seafood entrées, all accompanied by a wide choice of vegetables, yeasty little hot rolls and tiny blueberry muffins. Most foods are grilled, sautéed, baked, or broiled, without the addition of chemicals and heavy seasoning; it's REAL food, in an unforgettable setting.

Equally unforgettable are the homemade pies— the chocolate is dense and mousse-like— and Greek Karidopita, a light-textured ginger cake in a delicate rum sauce.

The Doak House, on TN 107 next to Tusculum College, just east of Greeneville, is open for lunch 11 a.m. to 2 p.m., and for dinner 5 to 10 p.m., Tuesday through Saturday. Hours are sometimes shorter during winter months. (615)639-4681. Dress is "comfortable," reservations are accepted, and are preferred for parties of 6 or more. MC, V. ($$)

DOAK HOUSE CREAM OF BROCCOLI SOUP

2 1/2 quarts chicken stock
1 1/2 cups chopped broccoli
1 1/2 teaspoons MSG
3 Tablespoons sugar
1/2 cup chopped celery
2 large carrots, chopped
1/4 large onion, chopped
1 quart milk
4 ounces butter
4 ounces flour

In large pot, combine first 8 ingredients and bring to a boil. Add milk and return to boil. Blend butter with flour and stir into mixture; when thickened, turn off heat. Serves 10 to 12.

DOAK HOUSE CRAB MEAT DRESSING
FOR STUFFED TROUT

6 hard rolls
1 stick butter
1/2 cup chopped celery
6 Tablespoons chopped
  onion
1/8 teaspoon sage

1/4 teaspoon salt
1/8 teaspoon white
  pepper
One 6-ounce can
  crab meat
1 Tablespoon white
  wine

Split and toast rolls. In blender or food processor, crush to coarse crumbs. In saucepan, melt butter, then sauté celery and onions until translucent. Add seasonings, then mix with bread crumbs. Add crab meat and wine, and blend well. Use to stuff trout or mushrooms.

DOAK HOUSE SALAD DRESSING

1/3 cup cider vinegar
1/3 cup white vinegar
1/3 cup water
1 cup oil
1/2 cup Dijon mustard
Heaping 1/2 teaspoon
  white pepper

1 teaspoon salt
Heaping 1/4 teaspoon
  garlic powder
1/3 cup + 2 Tablespoons
  sugar
1/2 teaspoon oregano

Blend all ingredients. Yields about 2 1/2 cups.

HALE SPRINGS INN
Rogersville

The first white settlers arrived in Tennessee in 1769; by 1772, there were settlements north of the Holston River. Thomas Amis, Captain and Commissary of North Carolina troops during the Revolution, built a stone house in 1780, followed by a store, forge, distillery, gristmill, and tavern, all before 1783. In 1785, when Mary Amis married Joseph Rogers, employed by her father as storekeeper, Amis gave the young couple the large tract of land that became Rogersville.

Situated on the Wilderness Road, Rogersville prospered from the first, attracting residents of every profession. John McKinney, a lawyer, came to Rogersville in 1800. The house he built in 1810 still stands, and Rosemont, ca. 1842, home of his daughter Susan and her husband John Netherland, adjoins the law office McKinney and Netherland shared.

In 1824, McKinney built McKinney Tavern, a massive three-story red brick structure designed by John Dameron, architect of the Hawkins County Courthouse, ca. 1836, the oldest courthouse in Tennessee.

Visited by the three Tennessee presidents, Jackson, Johnson, and Polk, the Inn was popular for generations. It was patronized during the War Between the States by Union sympathizers; Confederates used Kyle House, across the street.

The name McKinney Tavern was changed to Hale Springs Inn in the 1880's, when it was a stop for travelers to Hale Springs resort. The oldest continuously operating Inn in Tennessee, it was placed on the National Register in 1973, as part of the Rogersville Historic District.

Captain Carl Netherland-Brown, descended from builders of the Netherland Inn in Kingsport, and related to the original owners of Rosemont, had just restored Rosemont when he was encouraged to restore the Inn in 1982.

Despite demolition required by an unfortunate 1930s "modernization," in which false walls divided the rooms, and an ugly 1940s wing, the Inn never closed during restoration. Today, there are eight spacious guest rooms, including two suites, each with modern plumbing and a wood-burning fireplace.

Wide halls on each floor are brightened by windows at each end, showing off the original heart-pine floors. Antique furnishings have been used wherever possible (beds and wing chairs are comfortable reproductions) and the Inn houses a collection of paintings by one of Tennessee's best-known early portraitists.

On the first floor, the former dining room serves as kitchen; the original taproom is now the Colonial Dining Room, where firelight and candles create a subdued atmosphere, and waitresses in colonial dress present food designed for modern tastes.

Chef Ed Queener said, "I hope guests are pleasantly surprised at the diversity of the menu in a little town like this. Just about everything is homemade."

It's also very good and attractively presented, and changes to reflect the seasons. There's a special soup every lunch and dinner— Tomato Florentine with spinach and noodles is the favorite— and fresh pasta and a catch of the day every evening. Light, unusual luncheon entrées such as Chicken Lasagna and Cajun Beans and Rice are served with vegetable, plus potato salad or cole slaw, and hearty sandwiches come with soup or salad.

Dinner features the house special Prime Rib with Yorkshire Pudding, or you might choose the Shrimp Kabob grilled with butter— and all entrées include soup, vegetable, starch, and a toasty loaf of homemade bread.

Desserts include homemade fruit cobblers, rich Chocolate Decadence cake with whipped cream and raspberry purée, or wonderful Peach Schnapps Ice cream.

Do you suppose Andrew Jackson ate this well?

Hale Springs Inn, 110 W. Main Street, Rogersville, is open for lunch 11:30 a.m. to 2 p.m., Tuesday through Friday, and for the Sunday Buffet. Dinner is 6 to 9 p.m., Tuesday through Saturday. (615)272-5171. Reservations are preferred, and are required for parties of ten or more. Busiest time is Heritage Days, the 2nd weekend in October, often booked a year in advance. AE, MC, V. ($$)

HALE SPRINGS INN VEAL OSKAR

For each serving:

Veal cutlets, floured	**3 asparagus spears**
CLARIFIED butter	**Chunks of crabmeat**
	Bearnaise sauce*

44

In skillet, sauté cutlets in CLARIFIED butter until medium rare. Place cutlets on heated plate, top with asparagus spears, alternating with chunks of crabmeat. Cover with Bearnaise sauce and brown slightly under broiler.

*Most general cookbooks have a recipe for this classic sauce.

HALE SPRINGS INN YORKSHIRE PUDDING

Beef drippings	**Salt and pepper**
2 cups milk	**2 cups flour**
4 eggs	

Coat muffin tin cups with drippings and place in 450 degree oven for 5 minutes. Meanwhile, in mixing bowl, combine milk with eggs and seasonings, and whip in flour until smooth. Fill heated tins 3/4 full. Reduce heat to 250 degrees and bake 15 to 20 minutes or until pudding is fluffy. Serve immediately with any beef entree. Yields 12.

HALE SPRINGS INN CHOCOLATE DECADENCE

1 pound baking chocolate	**Brandy**
	1/4 cup flour
6 ounces butter	**Whipped cream and**
4 eggs, separated	**raspberry purée for**
3/8 cup sugar	**garnish**

Oil and flour 10-inch springform pan. In double boiler over simmering water, melt chocolate with butter. In mixing bowl, whip egg yolks with sugar until smooth, then blend into chocolate mixture, adding a splash of brandy. Cool mixture. In mixing bowl, whip whites until stiff, and fold whites and flour into chocolate. Pour into prepared pan and bake 15 minutes at 450 degrees. Cool completely. Garnish with whipped cream and raspberry purée. Yields 16 servings.

THE ATTIC RESTAURANT
Talbott

Long before white men came to Tennessee, Mound Builders and Indians raised corn in the fertile valleys. Farming became the chief occupation of settlers, with corn's related products of bacon, lard, and corn whiskey being the first agricultural exports.

Farms in East Tennessee, limited in size by the terrain, were nearly self-sufficient—practically every necessity could be grown on the place or made from materials near at hand—but farmers had little cash. Four years of The War Between the States, followed by reconstruction, left them in perilous condition, and it was the first decade of the twentieth century before the value of farm property returned to respectable levels.

Truck farms and orchards became profitable, hog raising continued to be important, and poultry and egg production increased, making Morristown one of the largest poultry-shipping centers in the country.

At nearby Talbott, a farm on the Hamblen/Jefferson county line is believed to have belonged first to a Dr. Brown, who lived and practiced in a one-room log cabin. About 1847, a large farmhouse was built in front, possibly by a rural mail carrier named John May. The property stayed in his family until mid-twentieth century.

When Mildred and Frank Pokorny bought it in 1975, the house had stood empty for years. They restored it for use as a gift shop, with a small tea room, but demand for Mildred's cooking was so enthusiastic that a new dining room was added in 1982. Gifts and crafts are now in four upstairs rooms and in the adjacent outbuildings; the Pokornys live in Dr. Brown's cabin.

A cheerful yellow, trimmed in white, The Attic nestles in tall trees, and overlooks beautiful rolling land. Waitresses in long calico dresses and white aprons deliver the kind of tearoom food that men enjoy as much as women do.

Menus change every two weeks, but lunch always includes homemade soups, salads, crêpes and the County Line Platter, which might be homemade lasagna or Green Bean Almondine, a specialty of the Pokorny's daughter, Nancy Meinert.

Dinner offerings, accompanied by cheese and crackers, a cup of soup, salad, and homemade rolls, are baked, broiled, or sautéed. "We have very little fried food," said Mildred. Special is baked

47

Chicken Washington, with cheese and mushrooms, and Beef Tenderloin Tip Crêpes with mushroom sauce.

Desserts at both meals are mouth-watering: Turtle Cake, Reese Cup Pie, Carrot Cake, Apricot Amaretto Cake, and The Attic's rich, dense Peanut Butter Pie in a flaky homemade crust, topped with whipped cream.

The Attic is on US 11E, 3 miles east of Jefferson City and 8 miles west of Morristown. (615)475-3508. Lunch is served from 11 a.m. to 2:30 p.m., seven days a week, and dinner from 5 to 9 p.m. every day except Sunday. Dress is casual, and reservations are accepted, preferred for groups of 8 or more, and probably necessary during October. AE, MC, V. ($$).

THE ATTIC TRIPLE DECKER CHICKEN SALAD SANDWICH

8 cups chopped cooked chicken
1 cup diced celery
1 carrot, shredded
1 medium onion, grated fine
1/2 teaspoon salt
1 teaspoon Beau Monde seasoning

1 cup to 1 1/2 cups mayonnaise
12 slices white bread
Cream cheese icing (below)
4 slices canned pineapple
4 maraschino cherries

In large mixing bowl, blend first 6 ingredients, adding mayonnaise to achieve the proper texture. Cut large rounds from bread slices, and, for each sandwich, spread 2 with chicken salad, stack, and place plain round on top. Spread sides with cream cheese icing. To serve, place sandwich on large lettuce leaf, top with pineapple slice and cherry. Yields 4.

For cream cheese icing, blend 2 8-ounce packages cream cheese with 1/4 cup pineapple juice until smooth and spreadable.

THE ATTIC PUMPKIN BREAD

3 1/3 cups flour
2 teaspoons baking soda

4 eggs
2 cups pumpkin (1 can)

1 1/2 teaspoons salt
1 teaspoon cinnamon
1 teaspoon nutmeg
1 cup vegetable oil

2 2/3 cups sugar
1 cup raisins
2/3 cup water

Combine dry ingredients and set aside. In mixer bowl, beat oil, eggs, pumpkin and sugar at medium speed. Blend raisins and water in blender until raisins are chopped. Add raisin mixture to ingredients in mixer, then add dry ingredients slowly until blended. Pour into 2 greased and floured loaf pans and bake 45 or 50 minutes at 350 degrees. Yields 2 loaves.

THE ATTIC PEACH SCHNAPPS CAKE

1 cup margarine, at room
    temperature
2 1/2 cups sugar
6 eggs, at room
    temperature
1 cup sour cream
1 teaspoon vanilla
    extract
1 teaspoon orange
    extract

1 teaspoon lemon extract
1 teaspoon peach extract
3 cups flour
1/4 teaspoon baking soda
1/2 teaspoon salt
1/4 to 1/2 cup peach
    schnapps
Glaze (below)
Sliced Almonds

Grease and flour 10-inch tube pan. Cream margarine and sugar until fluffy, adding eggs 1 at a time, beating well after each. Beat in sour cream, then extracts. Sift dry ingredients together, then add gradually. Beat in schnapps, pour into prepared pan and bake at 350 degrees 1 hour 15 minutes, until cake tests done in center. Cool 5 minutes, turn out on wire rack and cool.

Glaze and sprinkle with sliced almonds.

For glaze, blend one 8-ounce jar peach preserves with 1 Tablespoon peach schnapps and a dash of peach extract.

THE WONDERLAND HOTEL
Elkmont, Gatlinburg

T̲ennessee's earliest residents were prehistoric Indians: wandering tribes, mound builders, hunters and farmers. Of the historic Indians who passed through, the Cherokees had the longest tenure, making their homes in the mist-shrouded mountains of what is now Southeastern Tennessee, and hunting all over the eastern part of the state.

They hunted and fished, but took no more than they needed from the forests; early whites, in their greed, destroyed entire species, and forced the Indians from their land. The earliest settlers lived much as the Indians had, but as their numbers grew and settlements expanded into towns, the forests grew smaller and smaller.

Then the lumbering began. Railroads and sawmills were built, and trees were cut without regard for long-range effects. Fires erupted in unprotected undergrowth and erosion washed away topsoil.

In 1926, prompted by conservationists in Tennessee and North Carolina, President Coolidge signed a bill to create the Great Smoky Mountains National Park. Private contributions and government grants raised money to buy land, and on June 15, 1934, Congress authorized full development of the park.

Some virgin timber remained; second-growth timber has covered stripped forests and abandoned logging towns, fished-out streams have been re-stocked, and wildlife has multiplied. The mountains are not as they were before man, but they are as close as modern man can make them.

In the rugged beauty of the mountains, the musical turmoil of the clear streams, and the dignity of the forests, visitors can imagine what this continent was like before man, and why the Indians believed the Smokies to be sacred.

Overlooking the Little River near Elkmont, the Wonderland Hotel is the only hotel in the Great Smoky Mountains National Park. Built in 1912 for visitors who arrived by rail, it became a private club in 1919, with an annex constructed the following year. The hotel was then opened to the public as well as to members. When it was purchased by the Park, owners were given a lease arrangement that expires in 1992; at that time, it, too, will be returned to nature.

Until then, this rustic hostelry evokes the relaxation of an earlier time. The two-story frame building is surrounded by wide porches under shady trees. Twenty-seven rooms upstairs are cooled by mountain breezes, and there's usually an open fire in the lobby and the dining room. Here, country breakfasts prepare visitors for a day's fishing, hiking, or sitting in a porch rocker.

For lunch and dinner, there's flaky, tasty, broiled mountain trout, country ham, and fried chicken, with sandwiches and salad bar for lighter appetites. They'll even cook the fish you catch, if you clean them. Homemade cobblers, blackberry, peach, apple, or cherry, are full of berries under a perfect crust.

"We don't do anything fancy," said Darrell Husky, hotel manager since 1979. "We try to stick to the basics, like going to grandma's house." He knows his clientele: about 85 per cent are repeat visitors, who "come here to unwind, get away from the television, the telephone, and the rat race."

Husky plans activities to bring guests together: watermelon cuttings, making homemade ice cream, building fires to sit around. There are ping-pong and card tables in the lobby and acres of forests and streams outside, and that wonderful porch to sit on and rock.

"The first time here," Husky said, "you're a guest. From then on, you're more like family."

The Wonderland Hotel is open from early May until November 1. To reach it, take US 441 from Gatlinburg 2 miles to Sugarland Visitors Center. Turn right on 73W, and drive about 6 miles toward Cades Cove, watching for signs. (615)436-5490. Dress is casual, and dining room hours are 7:30 a.m. to 8:30 p.m., with continuous service. Dining room reservations are only accepted for parties of 15 or more; hotel reservations are necessary, and are accepted from November 15 for the following summer. October is the busiest month. MC, V. ($$)

WONDERLAND HOTEL
THOUSAND ISLAND DRESSING

1 cup mayonnaise
1 cup bottled chili sauce

1 teaspoon chopped green pepper

1 teaspoon chopped
   onion

2 boiled eggs, chopped
1 teaspoon celery salt
Salt and pepper

Blend all ingredients. Chill 1 to 2 hours before serving.

WONDERLAND HOTEL COUNTRY "CAT HEAD" BISCUITS

2 cups self-rising flour
1 cup vegetable
   shortening

1 Tablespoon baking
   powder
1 cup buttermilk

Sift flour; blend in remaining ingredients. Knead on floured surface, pat out about an inch thick and cut with large biscuit cutter. Place on buttered baking sheet and bake at 400 degrees until brown. Serve hot with butter and honey. Yields about 18.

WONDERLAND HOTEL BLACKBERRY COBBLER

2 cups fresh or frozen
   berries
1 1/2 cups butter or
   margarine, divided

1 1/2 cups sugar, divided
2 cups self-rising flour
Cold water
Melted butter

Place berries in bottom of baking pan. Melt 1/2 cup butter and pour over berries. Sprinkle with sugar, reserving 5 Tablespoons. Sift flour and work in remaining 1 cup butter until mixture is like coarse crumbs. Add enough cold water to make mixture form a ball (about 6-8 Tablespoons). Knead on floured surface; roll out thin; cut strips and place over berries. Sprinkle with remaining sugar and melted butter. Bake at 400 degrees until brown. Serve hot with ice cream.

APPLEWOOD FARMHOUSE
RESTAURANT
Sevierville

Of all the colorful, romantic characters in Tennessee history, one man dominates the imagination. Tall, handsome John Sevier (pronounced Se-VERE) was among the area's first settlers, and took part in nearly every activity that shaped the territory and the state.

A Virginian of French Huguenot descent, Sevier was brave, quick to make friends, and a natural leader. He was an Indian-fighter, hero of the Battle of King's Mountain, Governor of the State of Franklin, General of Militia of The Southwest Territory, four-term Representative to the U.S. Congress, first Governor of Tennessee, and served five additional terms as Governor.

Sevier County, and its seat, Sevierville, are both named for this dashing patriot. Some of the loveliest country in the state, Sevier County is changing from farming country into a tourism center; in keeping with this trend, an unusual restaurant has been developed on a farm overlooking the Little Pigeon River.

Cattle and tobacco were raised on the farm by owners Bill and Georgia Kilpatrick and Bon and Nancy Hicks, but an apple orchard, begun in 1976, proved better use of the land. In 1980, the barn was cleaned and converted to The Apple Barn and Cider Mill, a retail outlet for apples and a variety of country foods and crafts.

A 1986 partnership with Jim Huff has resulted in expansion of the 1921 farmhouse to six dining rooms, each with a distinctive personality. White furniture and swings furnish porches overlooking the orchard, and homey pine outfits keeping room and country kitchen.

The original living and dining rooms are furnished in oak, to match the beautifully crafted mantel, room divider, and built-in cupboards made by Louis Buckner, a black artisan born in slavery. By 1880, he was listed as a cabinetmaker, but in addition to furniture, he built some of the finest houses in Sevierville, including two listed on the National Register.

The Applewood Farmhouse Restaurant features, of course, apples— apple juice, tiny hot applesauce muffins, and apple butter appear on your table before you order— but there's plenty of variety, and everything is down-home good. Meats— such as beef brisket and baby back pork ribs— are smoked on site, and all pies and baked goods are homemade.

Hearty country breakfasts provide everything from country ham to buttermilk pancakes, and lunches can be fried chicken, fruit salads, sandwiches on homemade bread, or "Farmburgers" such as Salmonburger, Porkburger, and Turkeyburger.

Dinner adds entrées of chicken-fried steak, barbecued spareribs, and rainbow trout, with plenty side dishes, but at all meals, be sure to save room for dessert: apple cake, apple roll, caramel cream pie, even a chocolate fudge cake, and the remarkable Applewood Pie-Cake, a dense apple-walnut spice cake, topped with whipped cream and rum sauce.

Applewood Farmhouse Restaurant is on Lonesome Valley Road, Sevierville, and is open 8 a.m. to 9 p.m. Sunday through Thursday, to 10 p.m. Friday and Saturday, with continuous service. (615)428-1222. Dress is casual, and reservations are not accepted, except for groups of 10 or more. Busiest time is September (Apple Festival) and October. AE, MC, V. ($$)

APPLEWOOD FARMHOUSE APPLESAUCE MUFFINS

1 cup butter	4 cups flour
2 cups sugar	1 Tablespoon cinnamon
2 eggs, beaten	1 Tablespoon allspice
2 cups applesauce	2 Tablespoons vanilla
2 teaspoons soda	extract

In mixing bowl, cream butter and sugar; add eggs. Heat applesauce; stir in soda. Sift dry ingredients together and add to butter mixture alternately with applesauce. Add vanilla. Pour into greased muffin tins (or paper baking cups in tins) and bake at 350 degrees until light brown, about 15 to 20 minutes. Batter will keep, covered and refrigerated, for several days.

APPLEWOOD FARMHOUSE APPLE FRITTERS

1 cup milk	1 teaspoon vanilla
1 egg, beaten	1/2 cup sugar
4 Tablespoons	1/2 teaspoon salt
margarine, melted	3 cups cake flour

Juice and rind of one
orange
1 cup coarsely chopped
apple

2 teaspoons baking
powder
Oil for deep frying

In mixing bowl, combine milk, egg, and margarine. Add fruit and vanilla. Sift dry ingredients and stir into mixture only until blended. DO NOT OVERMIX. Preheat oil to 350 degrees. Drop fritters off end of tablespoon into hot oil and fry to a golden brown, turning to brown evenly. Drain and cool.

APPLEWOOD FARMHOUSE SPECIAL PIE CAKE

1/4 cup butter or
margarine, softened
1 cup sugar
1 egg
1 cup flour
1 teaspoon salt
1 teaspoon cinnamon
2 Tablespoons hot water

1 teaspoon vanilla
extract
3 cups peeled, diced
cooking apples
1/2 cup chopped pecans
Rum-butter sauce
(below)
Whipped cream for
garnish (below)

Cream butter, beat in sugar, then egg, and blend. Combine dry ingredients; add to creamed mixture and beat on low speed until smooth. Stir in water and vanilla, then fold in apple and nuts. Spoon into greased and floured 9" pie plate and bake at 350 degrees 45 minutes or until tests done. Serve warm or cold with Rum-butter sauce and (optional) whipped cream.

For Rum-butter sauce, blend 1/2 cup packed brown sugar, 1/2 cup sugar, 1/4 cup soft butter or margarine, and 1/2 cup whipping cream in a saucepan. Mix well, then bring to a boil and cook one minute. Stir in 2 Tablespoons rum.

For Whipped Cream, whip 2 cups whipping cream with 1/3 cup brown sugar and 1 teaspoon vanilla until stiff.

THE BISTRO AT THE BIJOU
Knoxville

$\mathbf{T}$he oldest commercial building in Knoxville dates from 1816, when Thomas Humes, a prosperous Irish-born merchant, began a three-story brick structure on the corner of Gay and Cumberland streets. Humes died before its completion, but his widow leased part of the building to a silversmith in early 1817, and the Knoxville Hotel opened in July of that year.

Advertisements in 1821 mention thirteen rooms, with barroom, ballroom and dining room, stables and outbuildings. Under various names and proprietors, the hotel was home and offices to many of Knoxville's early professional men, and was the center of social activity for generations.

In the 1850s, the hotel, re-named "Lamar House," was enlarged to accommodate 250 guests, and Gay street was graded and lowered, so that the hotel's basement became its first story; a new entrance and exterior remodeling created the façade that still exists.

After occupation by both armies during the War Between the States, popular Lamar House, still a social center, hosted a reception for President Rutherford B. Hayes in 1877.

In the 1890s, commerce moved toward the railroads, and the Lamar House declined. The rear of the building was demolished, and The Bijou Theatre was constructed in 1909, entered through the original building.

Legitimate theatre and vaudeville performances were followed by moving pictures at The Bijou, but by the 1960s, there were undesirables in the hotel and X-rated movies in the theatre. Both operations were closed, and in 1975 a "Save The Bijou" campaign was successful. The building was placed on the National Register in 1975.

Renovated as home for Knoxville's performing arts, the Bijou Theatre reopened in the fall of 1977; fund raising and rejuvenation have returned it to top condition.

In a portion of the original building's basement and an early one-story addition, The Bistro at the Bijou opened in 1982, where restaurants had been more or less continuously from the 1920s. Owned by Cliff and Jill Fry, and managed by Cynthia Reese-Foxworth, The Bistro is a popular stop for lunch or dinner.

A European environment is created by dark green ceilings and quarry tile floors, with lots of light from large street-level windows illuminating a shady lady over the bar. Luncheon blackboard specials offer soups— always French Onion, but others might be Black Bean, Cream of Cauliflower, or chili—plus quiche and fish of the day. Salads are always good, especially the Spinach with Honey/mustard Dressing.

At dinner, Chef Thomas Schneider's specials include pasta dishes such as Smoked Salmon or Primavera, with Chicken L'orange or Blackened Cajun Rib Eye, and fish with creative sauces. Homemade desserts might be Chocolate Amaretto Cheesecake, fresh fruit cobblers, or Deep, Deep Chocolate Cake: three layers, filled and frosted with whipped cream, coconut, and nuts.

The Bistro at The Bijou, 807 S. Gay Street, Knoxville, is open Monday and Tuesday 8 a.m. to 8 p.m., Wednesday through Friday 8 a.m. to 10 p.m., and Saturday 4 to 10 p.m., with limited service mid-afternoons. (615)637-9841. All beverages are served, dress is casual, and reservations are not necessary but are accepted, and are preferred for parties of 6 or more. AE, MC, V. ($$)

THE BISTRO SPICY CHICKEN GUMBO

1 baking hen
Carrots, celery, onion to flavor broth
2 sticks butter
1 clove garlic, minced
1 medium onion, chopped
1 green pepper, chopped
1 sweet red pepper, chopped

3 ribs celery, chopped
1/2 pound Italian sausage, in bite-sized pieces
2 cups crushed tomatoes
Seasoning mix (below)
3/4 cups raw rice
One 8-ounce box frozen okra

In large pot, place hen, broth vegetables, and water to cover. Simmer until chicken pulls off bones, about 2 hours, adding more water as needed. Strain and reserve stock; pull chicken from bones and set aside.

In another large pot, melt butter and sauté garlic until browned but not burned. Be careful! Add vegetables and sauté 5 minutes, then chicken pieces and sausage, and sauté 5 minutes. Add 3 cups chicken stock, and bring to a boil, stirring frequently. Stir in tomatoes and return to a boil. Add seasoning mix a teaspoon at a time, simmering 5 minutes after each, until desired spiciness is reached. Add rice and simmer until thickened, then add okra and simmer 30 minutes, stirring frequently to avoid scorching. If mixture is too thick, thin with additional chicken stock. Serve piping hot with lots of French bread. Yields about 16 servings.

For seasoning mix: blend 1/2 teaspoon EACH: salt, black pepper, cayenne, white pepper, thyme, oregano, and granulated garlic. Any left over may be used with other recipes.

THE BISTRO JACK NUT PIE

One 9-inch unbaked pie
  shell
1 1/2 cups pecans or
  walnuts
1/3 cup chocolate chips
3 large eggs, beaten

1 cup sugar
1/4 cup melted butter
1/2 cup Karo dark syrup
1 teaspoon vanilla
2 ounces Jack Daniel's
  whiskey

Place nuts and chocolate chips in pie shell. Blend eggs with sugar, then remaining ingredients. Pour mixture into pie shell, and allow nuts to rise to top of batter. Bake 1 hour at 350 degrees.

THE SOUP KITCHEN
Knoxville

In 1786, Captain James White built a log cabin on the west side of First Creek, and rapidly turned it into a provisioning place for Revolutionary soldiers who came to take up their land grants.

William Blount, Territorial Governor, arrived in 1790, and when streets were laid out and a town planned, he named the settlement for Henry Knox, U.S. Secretary of War, in an effort to acquire aid against Indian attack.

Knoxville slowly grew into a supply depot. As transportation improved, retail stores of a wide variety were established, and in 1853, land was given for a public market. In 1897, a large brick building was erected on the site, replacing earlier wooden structures.

Peter Kern, a German immigrant, settled in Knoxville and established a bakery on Main Street about 1872, and an ice house in 1878. By 1890, he was mayor of Knoxville, and had built a new, three-story bakery adjacent to the Market House.

The actual baking was done in the rear of the building; there was a soda fountain and salesroom on the first floor, and an elegant ice cream parlor and restaurant upstairs. Contemporary accounts mention crystal chandeliers, polished floors of Tennessee marble, and "nearly a dozen flavors of ice cream and sherbet."

Mr. Kern died in 1907, and after the business was sold in 1925, it was relocated. Several businesses, including a long-time meat market, were housed in the Kern Building, which was placed on the National Register in 1982.

After widespread concern for sanitation and a serious fire in 1959, the Market House was demolished. Today, Market Square is again an open air market, with fountains and shrubbery that make it a favorite noontime gathering spot.

In the Kern Building, a restaurant called "The Soup Kitchen" serves lunch to hundreds by utilizing a unique format: only soups, salads, and breads are sold, in a fast-moving cafeteria-style line. Even those with a half-hour lunch break can be assured of wholesome, delicious food, fast.

Bob and Jean Bardorf began in 1980 with a small restaurant in Oak Ridge that sold seven soups and one bread; they first expanded, then opened the Market Square branch, and are now franchising The Soup Kitchen in the Southeast.

What makes it special is three-fold: the first-class quality of the food, the homespun comfort of the restaurant, and the friendliness and enthusiasm of the staff.

Chili is always one of the seven or eight daily soups; others might be Snow Crab, Chicken Curry, Bayou Shrimp, Cheeseburger Mac, and Redskin Potato.

Four specialty salads are offered daily, and four or five breads, one of which is a sweet bread. Each comes on its own breadboard with knife and butter, and some of the favorites are brown, with oatmeal and bran; herb; cheddar cheese; apple nut; cinnamon pecan; and orange poppyseed.

The day's desserts might be chess bars, cheesecake, big fat chocolate chip cookies, and apple cake full of pecans and topped with a hot brown sugar frosting.

The only problem here is choosing, but if you're lonesome for one you especially like, just call up and name a day, and they'll prepare it for you and about a hundred of your best friends.

The Soup Kitchen, #1 Market Square Mall, Knoxville, is open 11 a.m. to 2 p.m., Monday through Friday. Carryout and delivery are available in downtown Knoxville. (615)546-4212. Dress is casual, bottled beer is served, and no credit cards are accepted, although personal checks are. Busiest time is during the Dogwood Arts Festival, three weeks in April. ($)

THE SOUP KITCHEN BELGIAN LEEK SOUP

1/4 pound bacon, cooked, drained, and diced
1 bunch leeks, coarsely cut
2 stalks celery, finely diced
1/2 teaspoon ground nutmeg
Butter for sautéing
4 cups chicken stock
1/2 cup flour
4 cups water
1/2 cup white wine
1 cup half and half cream
Grated provolone cheese
Croutons

In large pan, sauté first 4 ingredients until leeks are tender. Add chicken stock. Whisk flour into water, and strain into stock. Add wine and cream. Serve garnished with grated cheese and croutons. Serves 8 to 10.

THE SOUP KITCHEN SAVANNAH FISH STEW

1/2 pound diced onions
1/2 pound carrots, in
  julienne
1/2 pound yellow squash,
  in julienne
1/4 teaspoon thyme
1/4 teaspoon white
  pepper
2 Tablespoons olive oil

4 cups chicken stock
4 cups water
1 pound white fish
  (haddock, pollack, or
  turbot)
1 bay leaf
1 cup white wine
1/4 cup Pernod liqueur

In large pan, sauté first 5 ingredients in oil. When vegetables are tender, add remaining ingredients and cook until fish is done. Serves 8 to 10.

THE SOUP KITCHEN GRATIN SAVOYARD

6 Tablespoons butter
1 bunch leeks, coarsely
  cut
1/2 teaspoon white
  pepper
4 cups chicken stock

1/2 cup flour
4 cups water
1 pound cream cheese
1 pound vanilla yogurt
1 pound frozen chopped
  spinach

In large pan, melt butter and sauté leeks with pepper. Add chicken stock. Whisk flour into water and strain into stock. Add cream cheese and yogurt, and beat until smooth with wire whisk. Add spinach. Serves 8 to 10.

L & N Station

L & N SEAFOOD GRILL
RUBY TUESDAY
Knoxville

After the War Between the States and Reconstruction interrupted development as a "jobbing" center, Knoxville's boom resumed with the manufacture and distribution of textiles, leather goods, iron, and marble products. Large railroads were attracted, competing for freight and passenger traffic.

Completed in 1905, the Louisville and Nashville Railroad Terminal Station was considered the largest and finest station between Cincinnati and Atlanta. The "Chateauesque" brick building was designed under L&N's chief engineer, Richard Monfort, who built Nashville's Union Station.

Passenger service ended in 1968, and the station was used only for offices until 1975. Vacant and vandalized, it was purchased by Station '82 Ltd. in 1981, as focal point of the Knoxville World's Fair. It was placed on the National Register in 1982, and now houses two restaurants and offices for eight companies.

The original L&N Seafood Grill opened in March, 1982, and continues to serve twelve to fifteen varieties of fish, flown in daily. Everything is made from scratch and served in a pleasant high-ceilinged room and an enclosed verandah. In addition to grilled, broiled, sauteed, and fried fish, there are soups, salads and sandwiches at lunch, with appetizers and mesquite-grilled specialties at dinner. Pastas and piping hot biscuits served from the pan enhance both meals, and desserts are wonderful.

Ruby Tuesday at the L&N fits right into the former waiting rooms and ladies' dining room; Tiffany-style lamps and stained glass windows create an upbeat atmosphere. Food here ranges from quiche, soup, and salads to blackened New York strips and filets. Chicken Teriyaki is popular, as are the half-pound steak burgers, in eighteen varieties, and the all-natural salad bar and special desserts.

Balcony seating overlooking the fair site is seasonally available at both restaurants.

The L & N Station is at 401 Henley Street, Knoxville. Hours at the L & N Seafood Grill are 11:30 a.m. to 10 p.m. Monday through Thursday, until 11 p.m. Friday and Saturday, with continuous service. On Sunday, brunch is 11 a.m. to 3 p.m. and dinner 3 to 10 p.m. (615)971-4850. Hours at Ruby Tuesday are 11:15 a.m. to 12:30 a.m. Sunday through Thursday, to 1 a.m. Friday and Saturday, with one menu and continuous service. (615)971-4700.

At both restaurants, dress is casual, all beverages are served, reservations are accepted (preferred for 6 or more) and busiest times are during home football games and events at the fair site. AE, MC, V. ($$)

L & N SEAFOOD GRILL
NEW ENGLAND CLAM CHOWDER

4 1/2 ounces bacon, diced fine
12 ounces onion, diced
1 pound celery, diced
3/4 cup flour
Three 8-ounce cans chopped clams
1 quart clam juice
1 pound potatoes, in 1/2 inch cubes

1 Tablespoon Worcestershire
1 teaspoon Tabasco
1 3/4 teaspoons salt
3/4 teaspoon white pepper
3 1/2 cups milk
2 cups cream

In large pot, fry bacon over medium heat until crisp. Add onions and celery and cook until transparent. Stir in flour for 3 to 5 minutes. Drain clams, reserving juice. Add additional clam juice to make a quart. Stir juice into soup a little at a time, until smooth. Add potatoes and simmer until potatoes are tender and broth is thickened. If too thick, add more clam juice. Add clams and seasonings and simmer 5 minutes. Add milk in 3 stages, simmering between additions, then cream in 2 stages, simmering and stirring frequently to avoid scorching. Serves 20 as first course, 10 as dinner.

L & N CHOCOLATE TRUFFLE CAKE

1 pound semi-sweet chocolate
1/4 pound sweet butter

1 1/2 teaspoons sugar
1 teaspoon hot water
4 eggs, divided

In double boiler, melt chocolate and butter over simmering water. Stir in flour, sugar, and water, then egg yolks, one at a time, beating between each addition. Beat egg whites stiff but not dry, and fold into chocolate mixture. Grease bottom only of 8" springform pan; pour batter into it and bake at 425 degrees EXACTLY 15 minutes. Cake's center will be slightly underdone. Cool completely, wrap and chill. Serves 8.

RUBY TUESDAY CHICKEN SALAD

1 1/4 pounds boneless
 chicken breast
1 ounce onion, finely
 diced
4 ounces celery, finely
 diced
1/3 cup chopped hard
 cooked egg

1/2 cup mayonnaise
1 teaspoon Grey Poupon
 mustard
1/2 teaspoon black
 pepper
1 teaspoon seasoning
 salt
Juice of 1/4 lemon

In saucepan, poach chicken until JUST done. Chill in ice water no longer than 10 minutes. Cut into 1/2" cubes. Combine remaining ingredients, then fold in chicken.

RUBY TUESDAY FUDGE BROWNIE PIE

4 ounces unsweetened
 chocolate
1/4 pound butter
1/4 pound margarine
1 1/2 cups sugar
3 eggs

2 teaspoons vanilla
1/2 cup chopped pecans
1 cup flour
1 teaspoon baking
 powder

In double boiler over simmering water, melt chocolate with butter and margarine. Remove from heat; blend in sugar, then eggs, one at a time. Add 1/2 of pecans with flour and baking powder and beat until smooth. Spray 9" round pan with cooking spray, pour in batter, and sprinkle top with remaining pecans. Bake 35 minutes at 300 degrees; cool on rack. Do not refrigerate. Serves 8.

ANNIE'S
A Very Special Restaurant
Knoxville

When the East Tennessee and Georgia Railroad built a depot in Knoxville in 1855, it marked the beginning of a long and important involvement between the town and the railroads; Knoxville was the link between "The West" and Atlantic seaports. Raw materials— granite, hides, ore, produce— were brought in from the surrounding area, and finished products came from the East coast.

Wholesale distributors, called "jobbers," built warehouses along newly opened Jackson Avenue in the 1890s and early 1900s. These large structures had access to railroad sidings from the rear, and often elaborate showrooms in front. Here, visiting buyers selected items that would be retailed to purchasers in other towns.

With the decline of the railroads, many of the buildings were left empty; others were used for small retail operations, and by mid-twentieth century, the character of the district had changed. Some deteriorated buildings were demolished, while others, empty, were vandalized. When the Jackson Avenue Warehouse District was placed on the National Register in 1973, there was an increased awareness of its importance, but little actual improvement.

In 1983, Annie de Lisle opened a fine restaurant just north of the district, pioneering in bringing people to the area for food and quality jazz. Occupying half of a two-story building and its one-story addition, both dating from the 1920s, plus a seasonal courtyard, Annie's is the cornerstone of an increasing number of music and eating establishments in what has come to be called "The Old City."

Annie, a dancer who celebrated her seventeenth birthday in her first show, had done public relations and management work for another Knoxville restaurant before this undertaking, and sees many parallels between show business and the restaurant business.

"There's a lot of hard work in the daytime here," she said, "getting the flowers and lighting perfect. Then, at 6 p.m., the pink lights go on and the show is on."

That show business dedication to perfection is evident not only in the presentation, but in the quality of the food. "In a restaurant like mine," she said, "instead of doing the regular things every restaurant does, I've always tried to serve things people have never heard of."

With Chef Edward Krovicka, she does just that. Even the things that sound familiar often have an unusual quirk: meat pie is pork and vegetables with salsa and a crisp crust; black ravioli are stuffed with lobster and served with a yellow pepper sauce; and a chicken breast might be sautéed with basil, pine nuts, and white wine.

Menus change every three weeks or so, with old favorites in new guises and some new things to try. Guests are encouraged to suggest new items for the menu, and at Christmas, Annie offers some of her own English dishes, such as roast goose, poached salmon, and plum pudding flambé.

Everyday desserts are equally rich, with chocolate pâté, chocolate truffles, white chocolate mousse, plus tortes, cheesecakes, etc., and Annie's signature dessert, "Chocolate Decadence," is a sampler of everything chocolate on the menu.

Annie's, a Very Special Restaurant, is at 106 N. Central Avenue, Knoxville; exit off I-40 at the Business Loop, exit at Summit Hill Drive, then turn right at Central. It is open for dinner, Tuesday through Sunday, at 6 p.m.; closing times vary. Sunday lunch is served from 12 Noon to 2 p.m. (615)637-4484. All beverages are served, bar menu is available at all hours, and reservations are necessary on Friday and Saturday. AE, MC, V. ($$$)

ANNIE'S RED RIVER SOUP

2 pounds sweet juicy tomatoes
2 large juicy oranges (juice and pulp)
1 1/2 cups canned tomato juice
Pinch each: salt, pepper, celery salt
1 Tablespoon orange juice concentrate
3/4 cup chopped celery
Squeeze of lemon juice
Celery sticks and thinly sliced orange for garnish

In boiling water, blanch whole tomatoes; remove from water and cool. Peel and core tomatoes and remove seeds. Purée tomato pulp, add juice and pulp of oranges, canned tomato juice, and seasonings. Cook on low heat for 20 minutes. Do not boil. Remove from heat, add orange juice concentrate, and cool. Add chopped celery and lemon juice, and refrigerate at least 1 hour before serving. Garnish with celery sticks and orange slices. Serves 4.

An Annie's note: For an extra touch on an extra hot day, add a couple of ice cubes to each dish before serving.

ANNIE'S CHOCOLATE PÂTÉ

6 ounces semisweet
  chocolate
6 ounces bittersweet
  chocolate
1 2/3 cups heavy cream
5 Tablespoons unsalted
  butter
2 teaspoons Amaretto,
  OR

1/4 teaspoon almond
  extract
1 1/4 cups chopped
  (medium fine),
  blanched, toasted
  almonds
Cherries

In a double boiler, melt chocolate over hot water. In a saucepan, heat cream until scalded, stirring constantly. When cream is just about to lift up into a boil, remove from heat. Add chocolate and butter to cream, stirring briskly with a heavy spoon until chocolate cools and thickens somewhat. Stir in liqueur, nuts, and cherries. Line a small pâté or cheese crock with plastic wrap, spoon chocolate mixture in, and smooth surface. Press plastic wrap directly onto the surface of the chocolate. Place in freezer until hard, preferably overnight. Warm slightly before serving; to serve, slice with a warm, sharp knife.

MANHATTAN'S
Knoxville

Even before the Warehouse District was developed, saloons and taverns catered to the people who worked in the area's small mills and manufactories. In the 1890s and later, when each warehouse had its "street drummer," whose job was selling his firm's goods to traveling buyers, a better class of restaurant was needed. An early equivalent of today's "business lunch" put the buyer in a receptive mood, or thanked him for his order.

About 1900, on the southwest corner of Jackson and Crozier (now Central) a one-story, multi-purpose building was erected, with five storefronts facing Central Street. The corner store, according to tradition, was always a restaurant, and served spirits except during prohibition, which came to Knoxville in 1907. In the 1940s, a Greek immigrant named Cavalaris opened it as a chili parlor he named "The Manhattan Café" for his first sight of the New York skyline. Later, it was a drugstore, a small grocery, and a used furniture store.

When contractor Benny Curl bought it in 1986, the little building had been gutted by fire; its roof was missing, and floors had been ruined by weather, but months of loving rejuvenation brought it to habitable status.

Parts of other old buildings were used in its repair, including floors from the Golden Dragon restaurant, tables of yellow pine from an old tavern, and benches made of cutting tables from John Daniel's tailoring shop next door. Plaster was removed from the brick walls, and openings were made into the adjoining store; "porthole" windows on the Jackson Avenue side were uncovered, and a skylight was constructed on the new roof.

The result was an open, airy, modern space with an old feeling, and Curl's partner, Frank Snowden, brought his years of restaurant experience to create just the right menu for "Manhattan's," which opened in September, 1986.

It is a friendly neighborhood bar, with music that ranges from jazz to blues to rock 'n' roll, presented nightly in the side room. In both rooms, there is an atmosphere in which elderly ladies on an outing and construction workers are equally at ease, enjoying food that appeals to all tastes. "Everything you order is made right then," Snowden said, "we can leave out or add ingredients for special requests."

Popular menu items such as Fish and Chips, Chicken Enchiladas, and fat handmade burgers are joined by such lunch specials as Meat Loaf and Mashed Potatoes, or a diet Grilled Chicken Breast with cottage cheese and fruit. Dinner Specials might be Seafood Alfredo, Grilled Swordfish (or other catch of the day) or Chicken Stir Fry.

Manhattan's desserts are constantly changing, but usually include Amaretto Cheesecake and German Chocolate Cake, with pies and cobblers made from fresh fruits in season.

Manhattan's, 101 South Central Street, Knoxville, may be reached from I-40 by exiting onto the Business Loop. Exit at Summit Hill Drive, then turn right at Central. It is open Monday through Saturday, from 11 a.m. to 12 Midnight, often later on music nights, and until 2:30 a.m. on weekends, with continuous service. (615)525-4463. All beverages are served, dress is casual, and reservations are not accepted. Busiest times are Friday and Saturday nights, depending on entertainment. AE, MC, V. ($)

MANHATTAN'S RED BEANS AND RICE

1 pound dried red beans
1/2 large green pepper, chopped
1/2 large onion, chopped
1 cup chopped scallions
Butter for sautéing

1-1/2 teaspoons garlic, chopped
3/4 teaspoon red pepper
3/4 teaspoon salt
1 pound chopped ham
1/4 pound butter
Cooked rice

Cook beans in water to cover. Sauté vegetables in butter; add to beans with seasonings, ham, and butter, and simmer 2 hours, adding additional water, if necessary to keep from sticking. Serve over cooked rice. Serves about 15.

MANHATTAN'S MARINATED PORK CHOPS

Marinade:
1/2 cup Jack Daniel's whiskey

1/4 cup olive oil
2 cloves garlic, crushed

76

2 Tablespoons lemon
  juice

Fresh ground black
  pepper

For each serving, marinate 2 thinly sliced center cut pork chops 24 hours in marinade to cover. Grill or bake until done.

MANHATTAN'S CHICKEN ENCHILADAS

For each serving:
1 cup white meat of
  chicken, diced
Dollop of sour cream
1 Tablespoon chopped
  green chilies

1 Tablespoon chopped
  onion
2 corn tortillas
Grated mild cheddar
  cheese
Purchased enchilada
  sauce

In small bowl, blend first four ingredients. Roll half of mixture in each tortilla, and place on ovenproof plate. Cover with grated cheese, pour enchilada sauce over, and bake 30 minutes at 350 degrees. Serve with black beans and marinated salad.

MANHATTAN'S PHILLY STEAK SANDWICH

For each serving:
4 ounces thinly sliced
  raw steak
2 Tablespoons green
  peppers, thinly sliced
2 Tablespoons onion,
  thinly sliced

Butter for sautéing
Hoagie bun
1 Tablespoon Tiger
  Sauce
Sliced provolone cheese

In skillet, sauté steak with vegetables until just done. Place on bun, top with ONLY 1 Tablespoon Tiger Sauce, and sliced cheese. Broil to melt cheese. Serve open-faced, with french fries.

HAWKEYE'S CORNER, TOO
Knoxville

Perhaps the greatest tragedy of the War Between the States was that all participants were Americans; animosities smoldered long after the conflict was over, and divided families and friendships were never reunited.

Sentiments in East Tennessee were strongly Unionist, and although Secessionists in Middle and West Tennessee voted the state out of the Union, East Tennessee kept representatives in the United States Congress.

In the early days of the war, East Tennessee was primarily under Confederate control. Union sympathizers burned bridges to hinder Confederate supply lines, but, except for raids by small bands, no Federal troops entered the area until the summer of 1863, as General A.E. Burnside approached Knoxville.

On June 19, 1863, a band of Union raiders, some of them local men, accosted Dr. James Harvey Baker, a non-combatant Confederate sympathizer, at his home on Kingston Pike. There had been an exchange of fire with a Confederate scouting party in the road, and the Federals perhaps believed Dr. Baker was hiding some Confederates.

Dr. Baker, preparing to leave, was armed, and after exchanging shots with a soldier, returned to his house, taking his wife, their two small children, Mrs. Baker's little sister, and several Negro children to an upstairs bedroom for safety. Repeatedly, he called out the window to assure the Federals that he was the only man in the house, and that he would surrender if his family would not be molested, but the Federals entered the house and fired two shots through the bedroom door.

When Dr. Baker opened the door and returned fire, he was shot, and as he lay dying in his wife's arms, the Federals entered the room and struck him with gun butts and bayonets.

Twenty-two year old Abner Baker returned to Knoxville after serving in the Confederate Army, and avenged his father's murder by killing the recently elected Postmaster/County Clerk, who had been one of the Union raiders. Dragged from his cell, young Baker was hanged without a trial by soldiers, on September 4, 1865.

Dr. Baker's house, a two-story red brick built in 1840, passed through a succession of owners and had stood empty two years before becoming Hawkeye's Corner, Too in November, 1982. A lot of structural repair was needed, but owners Charles Ericson and Tom Short, proprietors of successful Hawkeye's Corner near the University of Tennessee, retained the house's Victorian warmth. Open fires are welcome on chilly days, the glass-enclosed porte cochère is a bright, spacious dining room, and the bullet-riddled bedroom door hangs on the hall wall as a reminder of the house's tragic past.

Today, it is a cheerful, popular restaurant with food that is "a little different," Ericson said. "We don't stick to the standard dishes. We make all our own sauces, and use local poultry and fresh seafood."

Hawkeye's menu is fun to read— many dishes have amusing names, such as Pita and the Wolf (sautéed chicken breast in pita bread) and Jive Turkey (sliced turkey with avocado, bacon, and jack cheese on multi-grain bread). In addition to sandwiches, there are homemade soups, hearty salads, six-ounce burgers, and light entrées. A favorite is Chicken Picata, boneless chicken breast sautéed with garlic, mushrooms, white wine and lemon, covered with mozzarella.

Yammers™, thin-sliced homemade sweet potato chips, make a great beginning or accompaniment, side dishes are plentiful, and any dessert is a winner. Chocoholics will love the Chocolate Amaretto Cheesecake, and Hawkeye's ice cream sundaes must be seen to be believed.

Hawkeye's Corner, Too, is at 9000 Kingston Pike, Knoxville, and is open 11 a.m. to 12 Midnight seven days a week, with Brunch on Saturday and Sunday, and continuous service. (615)693-7098. All beverages are served. Dress is casual, and reservations are accepted, preferred for 10 or more. AE, DC, MC, V, Discover. ($$)

HAWKEYE'S APPLE WALNUT CHICKEN

For each serving:

1 ounce margarine
4 ounces chicken breast strips
Flour, seasoned with salt and pepper

1 ounce raisins
5 slices apple, with peel
2 ounces English walnut pieces

4 ounces Apple Walnut	4 ounces cooked rice
Sauce (below)	Fresh fruit and endive
	for garnish

In skillet, melt margarine. Dredge chicken strips in seasoned flour and sauté; when about 3/4 done, add Apple Walnut Sauce, raisins, apple slices, and walnuts. When chicken is done and sauce has thickened to a glaze, pour over rice and garnish with fruit and endive.

For Apple Walnut Sauce: Stir together 4 cups apple juice, 1/2 cup Sherry, 3/4 teaspoon cinnamon, 1/2 teaspoon ginger, 1/8 teaspoon white pepper, pinch of thyme, and 3 ounces cornstarch. This must be thoroughly mixed and stirred; yields enough for 8 to 10 servings.

HAWKEYE'S HAVA BONANA

For each serving:

2 large slices banana	2 ounces chocolate
bread	syrup
2 ounces vanilla ice	2 ounces whipped
cream	cream
1/2 banana, sliced	Cherry for garnish

Place slice of banana bread on dessert plate. Top with ice cream and sliced bananas. Place other slice of banana bread on top to make a sandwich. Cover with chocolate syrup, whipped cream, and top with cherry.

THE COURTYARD CAFÉ
Cleveland

Threatened with invasion by hated British commander Patrick Ferguson, 1,000 Watauga settlers gathered at Sycamore Shoals in the Fall of 1780, prepared to carry the war to the enemy. In this ragged, ill-equipped, but determined group was born the volunteer spirit that has characterized Tennesseeans.

Inflamed by Reverend Samuel Doak's sermon, and joined by Colonel William Campbell and 400 Virginians, and Colonel Benjamin Cleveland and 350 North Carolinians, they pursued Ferguson to King's Mountain. There, on October 7, 1780, using Indian or guerilla tactics, they defeated Ferguson's army in one rainy hour. Patriot losses were minimal, and after a trial, they sent prisoners to Virginia and returned to their homes.

In gratitude to one of the heroes of King's Mountain, the Tennessee Legislature decreed that the seat of Bradley County be named for Col. Cleveland when it was established in 1836. Just a few blocks from the courthouse, in a Craftsman-styled frame bungalow, two creative women prepare healthful lunches and weekend dinners with a flair.

Indiana native Maxine Sparger, with her partner, Willie Gorentz, opened The Courtyard Café in February, 1988, after redecorating the little house in soothing colors consistent with its style. The living room in peach and gray provides waiting space before the fireplace (and the display case of spectacular desserts) as well as seating; the dining room is taupe and white, and the "Roman" room is black and white.

The courtyard from which the restaurant took its name is a shady flower-filled back yard, open seasonally.

Maxine and Willie take pride in serving freshly prepared, homemade food. Orange juice is freshly squeezed; cinnamon-apple, blueberry, or bran muffins are made every morning; mayonnaise is not used, and no fried foods are served.

Lunch at the Courtyard might begin with mushroom soup, a flavorful creamy broth with sliced mushrooms and a hint of cayenne, and go on to crab meat salad with sour cream-dill dressing, a hearty roast beef and cheddar sandwich with sour cream-horseradish sauce, or one of the daily specials.

At dinner, choose from three entrées that might be ten-ounce filet; leg of lamb; grilled barbecued shrimp, or a pasta dish. Included are soup, salad, and potato or vegetable.

Whatever they eat, ninety-five percent of the Courtyard's guests have dessert. It's no wonder, with an entire menu of favorites, plus seductive specials. Always offered is Ritz pie: meringue crust with Ritz cracker crumbs and pecans, surrounding chocolate mocha mousse. These desserts are as handsome as they are tasty— a guest, seeing the Chocolate Triple Layer Cheesecake, was so impressed he took a whole one home!

The Courtyard Café, 440 Worth Street, Cleveland, is open for lunch Tuesday through Friday, 11 a.m. to 3 p.m., and for dinner Friday and Saturday, 6 to 10 p.m. (615)472-7283. Dress is casual, although most men wear coats and ties, and reservations are highly recommended for lunch and almost required for dinner. V. ($$)

COURTYARD CAFÉ
ORIENTAL SALAD AND DRESSING

1 pound fresh spinach
One 8-ounce can sliced
 water chestnuts
One 15-ounce can bean
 sprouts

1/2 pound bacon, fried
 and crumbled
4 hard cooked eggs, cut
 up

Toss together. Add dressing just before serving. For dressing: combine 1 cup salad oil, 1 Tablespoon onion salt, 1/3 cup catsup, 1/4 cup vinegar, 3/4 cup sugar, and 1 Tablespoon Worcestershire in screw-top quart jar. Shake well before serving.

COURTYARD CAFÉ DUCK GRAND MARNIER

4 domestic ducks
8 cups fresh orange juice
Juice of 1 lemon
2 cups sugar
1/3 cup Grand Marnier
 liqueur

1 1/2 teaspoons
 cinnamon
1/4 teaspoon nutmeg
1/4 teaspoon ginger
1/4 teaspoon allspice

Rinse ducks, remove giblets (reserve for another use) and place on cabbage leaves or a rack in pan at least 2" deep. In large saucepan, combine all ingredients and simmer about 1 1/2 hours. Pour over ducks and bake at 375 degrees for 1 1/2 hours. Serves 8.

COURTYARD CAFÉ DOUBLE DIABLO

1/2 cup raisins, soaked
   overnight in
1/2 cup Scotch whisky
14 ounces semisweet
   chocolate
1/4 cup water
1/2 pound unsalted
   butter

6 eggs, separated
1 1/3 cups sugar
4 ounces cake flour
1 1/3 cups finely ground
   blanched almonds
Pinch of salt
Icing (below)

Grease 12" cake pan, line bottom with waxed paper, then grease and flour paper. In double boiler over simmering water, melt chocolate in water. Stir in butter a little at a time. Beat yolks with sugar until thick; stir into chocolate. Add flour and almonds, then raisins and whisky. Beat egg whites and salt until stiff but not dry. Mix some of egg whites with chocolate mixture, then stir chocolate gently into egg whites. Pour into prepared pan and bake about 25 minutes, or until cake just shrinks from sides of pan. Center should be moist. Cool in pan 10 minutes, then turn onto rack. Pour icing over cake, smoothing with a spatula.

For icing: melt 8 ounces semi-sweet chocolate in 1 cup heavy cream, whisking until smooth.

THE RADISSON READ HOUSE
Chattanooga

The area that is now Chattanooga was important as far back as prehistoric Indians. Lookout and Signal mountains and Missionary Ridge provided shelter and observation points, and the Tennessee River offered transportation, as well as protection.

Cherokee Indians used the area as a trading center, but the first permanent white settlement was not made until 1835. In 1838 a town was laid out and given a Creek Indian name meaning "rock rising to a point."

A trading center for salt, bacon, flour, iron, whiskey, and textiles, Chattanooga was on not only the Tennessee River and the stage road over the mountains, but, by 1849, a railroad to Charleston and Savannah.

After confirming that Chattanooga's Union Station would be built across the street, George Crutchfield established his hotel in 1847; the station was built in 1858. Crutchfield House appears in photographs of the War Between the States era, when it was used as a hospital. It burned in 1871, and another hotel, built on the site the following year, was called The Read House.

With an 1880s addition, The Read House occupied nearly a city block, and was the social center of Chattanooga for generations. In 1926, a new, ten-story brick structure in the Georgian Revival style was completed. Known for its accommodations and the cuisine of the Green Room, it also boasted the first known hotel coffee shop, which opened in 1935. Placed on the National Register in 1976, The Read House was extensively remodeled in 1987.

Under the direction of Executive Chef Jack Martin, the elegant Green Room offers a broad and unusual breakfast selection, a luncheon buffet, and a sumptuous Sunday Brunch that overflows into the walnut-paneled lobby. Dinner might include Huntsman's Pâté, velvety Brie Soup with Wild Mushrooms, Warm Duck Salad, and Calypso Grilled Swordfish, topped with citrus. Classic desserts such as Bananas Foster vie with lavish temptations on the dessert cart.

The Broad Street Bistro, in the former coffee shop location, is a bright art deco eatery with a newspaper-style menu that offers innovative foods from around the world, featuring grilled fish, Bistro Burgers, and do-it-yourself deli sandwiches. Appetizers and salads with clever names are substantial, and "Happy endings" include old fashioned ice cream treats, Dutch Apple Cinnamon Crisp, and a rich, spicy Sweet Potato Pecan Pie.

The Radisson Read House is at 827 Broad Street, Chattanooga, and has 150 overnight suites. (615)266-4121.

Green Room hours for breakfast are 6 to 10 a.m., 7 days, for lunch buffet Monday through Friday, 11:30 a.m. to 2 p.m., and for Sunday Brunch 11 a.m. to 2 p.m. Dinner, Tuesday through Saturday, is 6 to 11 p.m. Coat and tie are requested, as are reservations. ($$$)

Broad Street Bistro has food service Monday through Saturday, 11 a.m. to 12 Midnight, Sunday 4 p.m. to 12 Midnight. Dress is casual; reservations are requested for parties of 6 or more. ($$)

In both restaurants, all beverages are served, and busiest times are during musical and theatrical performances and major conventions. AE, CB, DC, MC, V.

RADISSON READ HOUSE
TOURNEDOS OF BEEF DIANE

**1/4 pound butter, divided
2 1/2 pounds tenderloin, in 3-ounce medallions
Flour, seasoned with salt and white pepper
Brandy or cognac
1 Tablespoon minced shallot
1 cup sliced mushrooms
Worcestershire
2 cups brown sauce or beef gravy
1 or 2 Tablespoons chopped chives or green onion
1 Tablespoon chopped parsley
1/2 cup heavy cream**

In skillet, heat 1/2 of butter. Dust meat with seasoned flour and brown in butter. Splash carefully with cognac, and set meat aside. Add remaining butter to skillet; sauté shallots until tender. Splash again with cognac, add mushrooms and Worcestershire to taste. When mushrooms are tender, add brown sauce, chives, and parsley. Stir in cream, return meat to sauce, and warm through. Serve 2 medallions per portion over rice pilaf, with sauce spooned over. Serves 6.

RADISSON READ HOUSE
LAMB CHOPS LYNCHBURG

12 single bone rib lamb
   chops
4 Tablespoons coarsely
   ground pepper (about)
1/4 pound butter, divided
Jack Daniel's whiskey
2 cups brown sauce or
   beef gravy

Worcestershire
Heinz 57 Sauce
A-1 Sauce
Chopped parsley
Pink, white, and green
   peppercorns
   (optional)*

Rub each lamb chop on both sides with black pepper. In heavy skillet, heat half of the butter, add lamb chops, and brown. Turn chops and very carefully flame with Jack Daniel's. Continue to cook, about 4 to 6 minutes for medium rare. Remove chops from skillet and keep warm. Melt remaining butter in skillet and flame again with Jack Daniel's. Add sauces, parsley, and peppercorns. Return chops to sauce, and serve 2 chops per serving with sauce on the side. Serves 6.

*Note: the longer the peppercorns cook in the sauce, the hotter they become.

RADISSON READ HOUSE
TORTELLINI À QUATTRO FORMAGGI
(PASTA WITH FOUR CHEESES)

18 ounces dried or
   frozen tortellini
1/2 pound butter
3 cups heavy cream
6 ounces parmesan

3 ounces gorganzola or
   blue cheese
6 ounces provolone
3 ounces fontina or
   mozzarella
White pepper

Cook tortellini in plenty of water until al dente. Drain and shock under cold running water.

In heavy pan, melt butter, add cream, and bring to boil. Simmer until reduced slightly. Stir in cheeses, season with pepper, add tortellini and warm through. Serves 6.

THE BUNGALOW
Chattanooga

After their defeat at the battle of Chickamauga in September, 1863, Federal troops retreated to Chattanooga, and were held under siege by General Braxton Bragg's Confederate forces. Bragg failed to attack, and General U.S. Grant arrived with reinforcements, increasing Federal forces to 60,000; Confederate forces numbered about 40,000.

Grant planned for General "Fighting Joe" Hooker to take and hold Lookout Mountain, while General W.T. Sherman crossed the Tennessee River and mounted Missionary Ridge. General George Henry Thomas was to connect with Sherman and clear the ridge.

On the night of November 24, 1863, in an almost total eclipse of the moon, Sherman attacked, but ran into difficulties. Thomas' men, held back until noon of the following day, were to create a diversion, but, without orders, and shouting "Chickamauga," they swept over the rifle pits and charged the heights, resulting in a Confederate rout.

Counting the Union "Army of the Tennessee" and the Confederate "Army of Tennessee," more Tennesseeans took part in battle around Chattanooga than in any other engagement.

Missionary Ridge is a quiet residential area, now, with only monuments to mark the thousands who fell there. Just under the brow of the ridge, a Craftsman-style bungalow, built about 1910, perches on the hillside. Called "The Bungalow, a very special restaurant," it lives up to its name in many ways.

Decorated in shades of plum and blue, with small-patterned wallpapers and crisp white trim, the house retains the cozy qualities of its period. The restaurant's intimacy, combined with the consistent quality of its food and the personalized service, have made it an occasion restaurant, while regulars return week after week.

Owner Nady Riad is proud of his distinctive food. "Everything is done here in this little restaurant from scratch—in front of me," he said. Sauces are prepared for each entrée individually, and homemade French bread and a lovely raisin pumpernickel are made on the premises.

Luncheon menu offers salads (Chicken Salad in Pastry with frozen fruit salad is one of the best), hearty sandwiches (Prime

91

and Cheddar on rye with potatoes parmesan), and hot casseroles (Shrimp with artichoke hearts and Mandarin orange salad) all with wonderful homemade breads.

Dinner entrées include the Bungalow's popular Filet Mignon, aged 17 to 21 days; grilled lamb chops; Flounder à la Veronique, with white grapes; several unusual chicken dishes, and specials that range from lobster to Cornish hen. All come with salad, homemade bread, and vegetables.

The house special Créme Brulée is a creamy, delicate custard with caramelized crust, but there are also chocolate mousse, two cheesecakes daily, and frequently "Gateau Riche" of vanilla ice cream, layered with chocolate mousse and topped with homemade almond brittle.

The Bungalow, 17 S. Seminole, Chattanooga, is one block off Brainard, and is open for lunch 11 a.m. to 2 p.m., Tuesday through Friday. Dinner is 5:30 to 10 p.m., Tuesday through Saturday. (615)698-7081. All beverages are sold, dress is casual (although 90% of men wear coats and ties), and reservations are encouraged. AE, MC, V. ($$$)

BUNGALOW SHRIMP AND HEARTS CASSEROLE

25 jumbo shrimp, shelled, cleaned, and cut in half
One 6-ounce can artichoke hearts
3 ounces butter
1 cup heavy cream
1 cup milk
1/4 cup Sherry

1 1/2 teaspoons Worcestershire
1/2 pound mushrooms, sliced thin
Salt, pepper, paprika
Bread crumbs, parmesan cheese, and parsley for topping
Sliced lemon twists for garnish

Divide shrimp among 5 individual casseroles or one large one. Add artichoke hearts. Combine other ingredients and mix well, pour on top. Sprinkle with blend of crumbs, cheese, and parsley. Bake at 375 degrees for 25-30 minutes; garnish with lemon twists. Serves 5.

BUNGALOW CHICKEN

For each serving:

One 8-ounce boned chicken breast	Cinnamon
	Triple Sec
Brie cheese	Brown Sugar
Green apples, sliced	Melted butter
	Mornay Sauce*

Place breast skin-side down. Pound flat. Top with 1/2" pieces of brie, brown sugar, and apple slices, then sprinkle with cinnamon, triple sec, and brown sugar. Roll in melted butter, place on cookie sheet, and bake at 350 degrees for 20 minutes, or until golden brown. Serve topped with Mornay Sauce.

*Most general cookbooks have a recipe for this classic sauce.

BUNGALOW SPICED TEA

2 quarts water	18 ounces pineapple juice
3 Tablespoons whole cloves	Juice of 12 lemons
3 large tea bags	6-ounce can orange juice concentrate
12 sticks cinnamon	
4 1/2 cups sugar	

In large pot, bring water to boil. In large strainer or cheesecloth bag, place cloves, tea bags, and cinnamon. Add this and sugar to hot water and allow to steep 20 minutes; stir to make sure sugar is melted. Remove spices and reserve for 3 more uses. Pour liquid into 3-gallon container, add fruit juices and water to make 3 gallons. Serve over ice. About 48 servings.

CHURCHILL'S
Chattanooga

The War Between the States left Chattanooga in dilapidated condition; earthworks and forts remained from the hostilities, streets were almost impassible in wet weather, and camp-followers lingered, unimpeded by corrupt politicians.

By 1870, the city government was in control, undesirables had left town, and business was on the increase, encouraged by good transportation and cheap labor. Chattanooga rapidly became a manufacturing center, with foundries, lumber mills, brick works, tanneries, and furniture factories thriving.

During the boom of 1888, four businessmen joined to build four connected commercial buildings, sharing a common rock-faced façade, at the corner of Broad Street and Seventh Avenue. Two of them occupied the building: James Trigg's wholesale grocery, and James Smartt's wholesale boot and shoe business; tenants shared the remaining space.

The building was purchased in 1918 by Sterchi Brothers Furniture Company, succeeded in 1939 by Fowler Brothers, a related furniture business. At that time, the building was remodeled, acquiring a pink granite façade and a modern interior in which dividing walls were removed and replaced with columns. Fowler Brothers closed the store in 1985; as the Trigg-Smartt Building, it was placed on the National Register in 1986.

Remodeled for multiple use, the building now has an open atrium, with wide interior stairs to the basement and columns soaring past the mezzanine to the second floor. Churchill's restaurant, opened by Lanny and Janie McNabb in 1987, occupies the left side of the building, and achieves the cozy elegance of an English club in a light-filled interior.

Here you'll find food with an English flair and an attention to detail that extends to fresh flowers and raspberries from the McNabb garden. "We customize every single meal," Janie said. "We try to please and try to hire people who feel that way too."

Lunch from the menu might begin with Cheese Fritters or Cream of Artichoke Soup, and continue with one of the entrée salads— perhaps Black Bean and Turkey, with coriander dressing, or Peanut Chicken in Belgian Endive. Among hot entrées are Chicken Pot Pie with Cornbread Crust and Beef Carbonade, served over noodles. Those in a hurry appreciate buffet lunch in the Bull and Bear Pub, in what is believed to be the original street level of the building. Churchill's extensive wine collection is housed on the former sidewalk, visible through stone arches.

Dinner appetizers include Smoked Trout in cream and Shrimp Anne Boleyn (headless, wrapped with bacon and broiled in chutney butter); there are special soups and salads, and entrées that range from Shrimp and Lobster to Norwegian Salmon with Spiced Nuts. Especially popular are Rack of Lamb, and Medallions of Beef and Veal. An almost overwhelming selection of homemade desserts is presented on a cart, as are cordials, liqueurs, and rare whiskies.

You don't have to be an English clubman to appreciate this kind of food and service!

Churchill's, 701 Broad Street, Chattanooga, is open for lunch Monday through Friday, 11:30 a.m. to 2:30 p.m., for dinner 6 to 10 p.m., Monday through Thursday, to 10:30 Friday and Saturday, and for Sunday Brunch Buffet 11:30 a.m. to 2:30 p.m. (615)266-4455. All beverages are served; large wine collection. Dress is casual in the pub; most men wear coats and ties upstairs. Reservations are encouraged, and are almost a necessity on Saturday evenings or on performance nights. AE, MC, V. ($$$).

CHURCHILL'S HOUSE SALAD

8 ounces cream cheese
4 ounces water
2 eggs
Juice of 1 lemon
8 ounces salad oil, divided
2 1/2 ounces red wine vinegar
4 Tablespoons fresh chives

2 ounces mayonnaise
2 Tablespoons sugar
1 1/2 teaspoons Worcestershire
1 1/2 teaspoons paprika
1 1/2 teaspoons salt
1 ounce chopped garlic
4 Tablespoons Dijon mustard
Trail Mix for garnish

Beat cream cheese until smooth; beat in water until mixture is pourable. In processor or blender, combine eggs, lemon juice, and 1/4 cup oil. Add remaining oil in slow, steady stream. Add remaining ingredients and cream cheese mixture, and blend smooth. Serve over Bibb and romaine lettuce, and sprinkle with trail mix.

CHURCHILL'S RED SNAPPER WITH GINGER

For each serving:

One 7-ounce snapper fillet

Seasoned flour for dredging

CLARIFIED butter for sautéing

1 ounce watercress

Ginger Butter (below)

Dredge snapper in flour and sauté in CLARIFIED butter. Braise watercress and place on plate, lay snapper on top, and top with 1 ounce Ginger Butter.

For Ginger Butter: in saucepan, mix 3/4 teaspoon powdered ginger, 2 1/4 teaspoons chopped shallots, 1 1/4 teaspoons lemon juice, and 2 Tablespoons white wine. Boil until reduced by half. Add 2 sticks (1/2 pound) butter and stir until melted; remove from heat and beat 1 minute. Yields enough for 6 fillets.

CHURCHILL'S BISQUE OF SQUASH AND APPLE

1 medium butternut squash, seeded and coarsely chopped

2 quarts chicken stock

2 Granny Smith apples, seeded and coarsely chopped

1 large onion, chopped

1 1/2 teaspoons rosemary

2 Tablespoons melted butter

2 Tablespoons flour

Salt and pepper

8 ounces heavy cream

In large pan, combine first 5 ingredients. Cover and simmer until very tender. Purée in food processor; return to pan. Blend butter with flour, add to mixture, and simmer 15 minutes. Season and add cream. Serves 8 to 10.

PERRY'S
Chattanooga

The East Tennessee Iron Manufacturing Company moved to Chattanooga in 1849, and the city's first foundry and machine shop were built, in time becoming the property of Thomas Webster.

In the 1870s, there was a boom in iron; furnaces, foundries, and machine shops manufactured everything from tubing to railroad cars. At the peak of the boom, about 1871, a small brick shed was built in the railroad district of Chattanooga, and was used as a machine shop, probably for Thomas Webster's foundry.

Outside pig-iron competition ended Chattanooga's iron industry, and in 1880, the little building was purchased by the East Tennessee, Virginia, and Georgia Railroad for use as a freight depot. When the ETV&G was absorbed by Southern Railway System in 1894, it continued in the same use, being expanded in 1898 with a two-story brick addition for office space. The Southern Railway Freight Depot was used by the railroad until the late 1960s; it was placed on the National Register in 1983.

Remodeled into a mini-mall of retail shops, offices, and eating places, the Freight Depot harbors under its wide eaves an unusual restaurant.

Partially enclosed by greenhouse walls and ceiling, canopied in soft pink, Perry's combines an open, airy feeling with "high tech" decor, centering on cases of fresh fish surrounding the open grill. Salmon, swordfish, steaks, and dozens of specialty items are grilled right in the restaurant; luscious desserts and Perry's trademark muffins are baked in a secondary kitchen.

Executive Chef Ali Zemrani's menu, tailored around the grill, is Continental in flavor. In addition to salads and sandwiches incorporating grilled chicken and fish, lunch offerings include an outstanding Back Bay Chowder, rich with chunks of seafood and bacon; wood-grilled hamburgers; and light entrées such as Cold Smoked Trout and Salmon with Bagel.

Dinner entrées— Swordfish with Lime Butter, Norwegian Salmon with Pesto, and Jumbo Shrimp with Tomato Mustard Cream—are unusual and popular, and justify a high-calorie dessert: a slice of cake full of chocolate chips, whiskey, and coconut, topped with Haagen Das ice cream and drizzled with Jack Daniel's whiskey.

Perry's, 1206 Market Street, Chattanooga, is open 11 a.m. to 2:30 p.m. for lunch, Monday through Saturday, and for Sunday Brunch. Dinner is 6 to 10:30 p.m., seven days a week. (615)267-0007. Dress is casual, all beverages are served, and reservations are preferred, especially for six or more, and are almost always necessary on weekends. AE, V, Discover. ($$$)

PERRY'S OYSTERS FLORENTINE

For each serving:

Butter for sautéing	2 Tablespoons Pernod
6 oysters	liqueur
1/2 teaspoon chopped	4 ounces fish Velouté
shallot	Sauce*
1/2 teaspoon garlic	Hollandaise Sauce*

In skillet, melt butter and sauté oysters with shallots and garlic. Flambé with Pernod, then add fish Velouté. Spoon into oyster shells and top with Hollandaise Sauce; run under broiler briefly to brown.

*Most general cookbooks have recipes for these classic sauces.

PERRY'S DRESSING FOR SPINACH SALAD

For each serving:

3 ounces unsalted butter	Pinch of minced garlic
3 ounces white wine	Juice of 1/2 lemon
2 Tablespoons pine nuts	Salt and Pepper
4 artichoke hearts	

Melt butter in skillet over low heat. Add other ingredients and bring to boil. Serve warm over fresh spinach.

PERRY'S MARINADE FOR TUNA STEAK
WITH SOY AND GINGER

For each serving:

4 ounces light soy sauce	4 ounces water
1 small ginger root, grated (2 Tablespoons +)	4 ounces honey
	1 scallion chopped (green part only)

Dissolve soy sauce in water, mix in other ingredients. Marinate each tuna steak about 2 minutes (not more) and grill to taste. Glaze tuna on each side with marinade while cooking.

THE CHATTANOOGA
CHOO CHOO
Vacation Complex
Chattanooga

The importance of the railroads to the development of Tennessee cannot be overstated. Called "arteries for the circulation of the commercial blood of the state," twenty-one railroads were under construction in the state in 1857.

Chattanooga's first railroad, the Western and Atlantic, reached the city in 1846, connecting it to Charleston via Atlanta. When the Nashville and Chattanooga Railroad was completed in 1854, the East Tennessee and Georgia the following year, and the Memphis and Charleston Railroad in 1857, Chattanooga was at the center of a railroad network that stretched across the South.

Rail lines, severely damaged during the War Between the States, were soon repaired and flourishing again. The Cincinnati-Southern Railway reached Chattanooga in 1880, and its Terminal Station, in a modified Beaux-Arts style, opened in 1909.

Under what was then the world's largest freestanding dome, soaring eighty-five feet above the floor, the impressive main waiting room was entered through what is still believed to be the largest brick arch ever constructed. The Terminal's convenience was paramount: there were no stairways, baggage rooms were nearby, and thirteen tracks came directly into the station, with covered "butterfly" walkways from the concourse.

For more than sixty years the Terminal served Chattanooga. During peak periods over fifty trains a day boarded passengers here, but traffic slowed during the 1950s, and the last train departed August 11, 1970. The station stood empty, boarded up and scheduled for demolition, when, in 1972, a group of 24 Chattanooga businessmen planned to turn it into a vacation complex.

The Terminal Station was placed on the National Register in February of 1973; The Chattanooga Choo-Choo opened in May of the same year.

Devoted to railroad history, the Choo-Choo is a thirty-acre complex of hotel and convention facilities, shops and museum-type attractions, and restaurants. Accommodation is provided in traditional hotel rooms, or on pullman cars decorated to evoke the period when wealthy businessmen had their own cars.

Reminders of the great days of railroading are everywhere: a statue symbolizing the "Train Baron" who pioneered in railroads, a replica of the 1880s Baldwin engine which first puffed into the station, and the world's largest HO gauge model railroad exhibit.

Passengers on one of the many excursion trains which visit the Choo-Choo, or others in a hurry, may purchase tickets for meals in the Trans-Continental restaurant in the former concourse area, now glassed in. Here you'll find salads and traditional Southern favorites.

The Station House restaurant, in what was once the baggage room, opens in the evening, and features steak, seafood, marvelous juicy barbecued ribs, and singing waiters and waitresses.

The Trolley Café provides three meals a day, poolside, including a buffet breakfast; The Silver Diner offers pizza to go, to eat in the sidewalk cafe, or on the train car; and the Wabash Cannonball is a club car.

Dinner in the Diner recreates the romance of train travel, with formal service in a dining car, and all the elegancies of the era of train travel.

If you're lucky, you might be present when an excursion train huffs in to the Choo-Choo. Hungry, weary travelers will scramble out, and refreshed, return to their train for the return trip. And once again, the old terminal rafters will echo the famous, nostalgic call, "all aboard."

The Chattanooga Choo-Choo Vacation Complex, 1400 Market Street, Chattanooga, has 365 overnight rooms, including 48 on train cars. (615)266-5000. Food is available at all daytime hours in its various restaurants; some are open until 11 p.m. All beverages are served at several facilities; dress is casual, except for Dinner in the Diner, where coat and tie are preferred. Reservations are required for Dinner in the Diner, and accepted (often necessary) at the Station House. All price ranges are represented by the various restaurants. AE, DC, MC, V.

CHATTANOOGA CHOO-CHOO CORN FRITTERS

3 cups flour
2 Tablespoons baking
    powder

3/4 cup milk
1 Tablespoon vegetable
    oil

1 1/2 teaspoons sugar
1 1/2 teaspoons salt
3 eggs, beaten

1 cup whole kernel corn,
  drained
Deep fat for frying
Powdered sugar

Sift first 4 ingredients. Mix eggs and milk and add to dry mixture; add oil and corn, and beat until blended. Drop heaping tablespoons into 350 degree deep fat and fry 2 to 3 minutes, or until golden brown. Drain on absorbant paper. Keep warm and serve with powdered sugar.

CHATTANOOGA CHOO-CHOO PEANUT BUTTER PIE

One 9-inch Graham
  cracker pie crust
Heaping 1/2 cup peanut
  butter
Scant 4 ounces cream
  cheese

1 1/4 cups powdered
  sugar
2 1/2 cups heavy cream
1/2 cup toasted almonds

Cream peanut butter with cream cheese until blended. Add powdered sugar and mix well. Whip cream until light and stiff, being careful not to whip into butter. Reserve some of cream for garnish; blend remaining cream into peanut butter mixture, with about 2/3 of almonds. Spread filling in crust, pipe or spoon remaining cream on top and sprinkle with remaining almonds. Chill before serving. Serves 8.

DIANA'S
Home of the Sweetest Buns in Town
Cookeville

In eighteenth-century towns, baking was done in bake-shops, where housewives could purchase bread, or take their own loaves and meats to be baked in large ovens. Isolated farms, where there might be several hundred workers, had bake-houses, and cooks who did the baking.

On the frontier, however, neither equipment nor flour were available. Cooking utensils were few and crude: a large iron pot for stews, a few wooden vessels, and perhaps some pewter plates. Large pieces of meat were roasted over an open fire.

Wild meat and cornbread were pioneer staples. Removed from the cob, kernels of dried corn were placed in a wooden mortar and pounded with a wooden pestle until finely ground. Mixed with water, the meal became Johnny cake (colloquial for "journey cake," because it traveled well), ash cake, corn pone, or mush, depending upon how it was prepared.

Cornbread in its various forms was the cheapest and most filling form of bread, but others were soon added: biscuits, rolls, loaf bread, and sweet breads for dessert or breakfast. Baking was a necessary part of life, but a respected skill, and a woman who could bake good bread was a popular hostess.

Returning to her Tennessee heritage after years in Detroit, Diana Lynch lived ten years in Cookeville before opening a restaurant and bakery in a quaint Gothic-revival cottage in August, 1987.

The house was built by Hickman Quarles, a descendent of Major William P. Quarles, whose 1805 settlement at White Plains marked the beginning of the town that would become Cookeville. Remodeled and enlarged several times, it is an ideal showcase for Diana's excellent baking.

Diana's opens early for those who want a continental breakfast with a fresh-baked cinnamon or pecan roll, or a slice of one of the warm coffee cakes, possibly Almond Buttercream Torte, Caramel Apple Twist, or Fruit and Cheese Braid.

The only meal served is lunch, when hungry guests cheerfully wait to be seated upstairs, downstairs, or out on the porch. The decor is country Victorian, and the food is just fine. You're greeted by a basket of homemade bread and butter; sandwiches are served on wheat, rye, or white homemade bread; and soups, salads, and quiches are all homemade from fresh ingredients, and change daily.

"I've been trying to do a seasonal menu," Diana said, "but the pot pies are so popular I can't take them off." No wonder; chicken pot pies are served in their own crock, topped with a flaky crust, and beef-mushroom turnovers are shaved roast beef in puff paste.

Perhaps the most popular dish is chicken salad, served in a cream puff, but it is rivaled by a dessert cream puff, filled with ice cream and drowned in hot fudge sauce.

If you're lucky, Diana will decorate a lovely basket of fresh breads and treats for you to take home— if they make it that far!

Diana's, Home of the Sweetest Buns in Town, 104 East Spring Street, Cookeville, is at the corner of Fleming Street. Take exit 287 off I-40; at the square, turn left on Spring and drive west one block. Bakery opens at 7 a.m.; lunch is 11 a.m. to 2:30 p.m., Monday through Friday; dessert is available 2:30 to 4:30 p.m. Hours may be expanding— call for information. (615)526-6967. Dress is casual, reservations are accepted for parties of 5 or more, and the busiest time is at Christmas. MC, V. ($)

DIANA'S BROCCOLI DIP

One 10-ounce package
  chopped broccoli
2 Tablespoons butter
1/4 cup finely chopped
  celery
1/4 cup minced onion
2 cloves garlic, minced
1/2 pound mushrooms,
  chopped

1 1/2 pounds Velveeta
  cheese
1/4 to 1/2 teaspoon
  crushed red pepper
1/4 to 1/2 teaspoon
  Tabasco
2 teaspoons

Cook and drain broccoli. In saucepan, melt butter; sauté celery, onion, and garlic; add mushrooms and cook almost dry. Add broccoli and cheese and cook slowly until well blended. Season to taste with pepper and sauces. Serve with cubes of fresh bread for dipping.

DIANA'S PERFECT WHITE BREAD

2 1/2 cups flour
1 package dry yeast
2 1/4 cups milk
2 Tablespoons sugar

1 Tablespoon shortening
2 teaspoons salt
3 1/4 to 3 3/4 cups flour

In large mixer bowl, combine 2 1/2 cups flour with yeast. In saucepan, heat next 4 ingredients until warm, stirring constantly. Add to dry mixture and beat at low speed for 1/2 minute, scraping sides. Beat 3 minutes at high speed. By hand, stir in enough flour to make a moderately stiff dough. Turn out onto floured surface, and knead 8 to 10 minutes, or until smooth and elastic. Shape into ball and place in greased bowl, turning once to grease top. Cover; let rise in warm place until doubled, about 1 1/4 hours. Punch down; turn out on floured surface; divide in half. Cover and let rest 10 minutes. Shape into two loaves; place in 8 1/2" x 4 1/2" x 2 1/2" loaf pans. Cover and let rise until doubled, 45 to 60 minutes. Bake at 375 degrees about 45 minutes. If tops brown too fast, cover with foil last 15 minutes. Remove from pans and cool on racks.

THE DONOHO HOTEL
Red Boiling Springs

From earliest history, mineral waters have been believed to have medicinal properties. Bathing in spas was thought to cure diseases of the joints; "taking the waters" could relieve internal disorders. Inevitably, mineral springs attracted the afflicted, and hostelries were constructed to house them.

No longer restricted to invalids, spas such as Carlsbad and Marienbad in Europe, and Bath, in England, became fashionable resorts.

In the late nineteenth century, there were more than two dozen mineral resorts in Tennessee. Typically, there was a hotel, a bathhouse, and a pump where people conversed while sipping the often unpalatable waters.

These were advertised, in the florid language of the day, to cure such exotic diseases as dyspepsia, torpidity of the liver, chronic malaria, and chills, and were frequently bottled and sold through the mail.

Near a settlement in North-central Tennessee, a bubbling spring produced water with a red sediment, which healed the eye condition of Shepherd Kirby in 1840. When word spread, others flocked to the area.

At Red Boiling Springs, there were reportedly fifty-two springs, producing five types of water, each with its own properties. Red water was allegedly effective for diseases of the urinary tract; Black, for the digestive tract, for "nerve exhaustion" and insomnia; White, for dyspepsia; Freestone was free of trace minerals; and Double and Twist, named for its effect if taken internally, was reserved for mineral baths.

The Red Boiling Springs resort reached its greatest popularity in the 1920s and '30s, when nine hotels and eight boarding houses were kept full. For entertainment, there were four bowling alleys, two dance halls, a theatre, a silent movie theatre, a swimming pool, and three restaurants.

By 1940, the resort had waned, and the flood of 1969 ended the town's reliance on tourism.

Of the three remaining hotels, the Donoho Hotel, built in 1914, is oldest. A massive two-story building of frame construction, it has 47 rooms, with wide verandahs on three sides. It was placed on the national register in 1986.

Since 1974, Edith and Patrick Walsh have offered good country cooking, family style, at big tables in the spacious dining room. Country ham is a big item here. "We sold two tons of Clifty Farms country ham in 1987," Edith said. Fried chicken is also popular, as are pork chops and roast beef, which rotate as entrées. Southern vegetables might be green beans, creamed corn, fried okra, sliced tomatoes, or whatever is fresh, accompanied by the hotel's irresistible hot biscuits. Dessert at dinner is more biscuits with honey; at lunch, there's fruit cobbler: cherry, apple, peach, blackberry, and sometimes plum.

The Donoho Hotel, East Main Street, Red Boiling Springs, is about 75 miles northeast of Nashville. It is open from about May 1 to October 1, depending upon weather. Breakfast is at 7:30 a.m. weekdays, 8 a.m. Sunday; lunch at 12 Noon, Monday through Saturday, and 12:30 p.m. Sunday; and dinner at 5:30 p.m. weekdays and Sunday, 6 p.m. Saturday. All meals are served PROMPTLY, and reservations are REQUIRED. Reservations are best for overnight stays, also. Two meals are included in overnight charges. Busiest times are July 4th weekend, Labor Day weekend, and the weekend following. No credit cards are accepted, although personal checks are. ($)

DONOHO HOTEL SOUTHERN FRIED CHICKEN*

2 fryer chickens, cut up   1/2 teaspoon ginger
1 cup flour   2/3 cup lard or
1/2 teaspoon salt   shortening
1/4 teaspoon pepper

Wash chicken and drain. Mix flour with spices, and coat chicken well. In skillet, heat lard until very hot; place chicken pieces in lard and fry on one side until brown, then turn and brown other side. Reduce heat, cover, and let cook slowly 10 to 15 minutes, or until done. Serves 8.

112

DONOHO HOTEL
HAM HOCKS AND BLACKEYED PEAS*

3 cups dry blackeyed
  peas
3 pounds smoked ham
  hocks
1 1/4 cups chopped
  onions

3 quarts water
1 cup chopped celery
1 teaspoon salt
1/8 teaspoon cayenne
1 bay leaf

Rinse peas. In 6-quart dutch oven, combine water and peas. Bring to a boil and simmer 2 minutes. Remove from heat, cover, and let stand one hour. Do not drain. Stir in remaining ingredients, bring to a boil, cover, and simmer until hocks are tender and beans are done, about 1 1/2 hours. Discard bay leaf. Correct seasoning. Serves 6 generously.

DONOHO HOTEL PINEAPPLE RICE*

1 1/2 cups converted rice
1 teaspoon salt
3 cups water
3 eggs, beaten
2 teaspoons vanilla

1/2 stick margarine
2 cups sugar
One 20-ounce can
  crushed pineapple

In saucepan, bring first three ingredients to a boil, stirring once or twice. Cover tightly and simmer 20 minutes. Remove from heat. Combine remaining ingredients and pour into rice, then pour into 11 1/2" x 7 1/2" x 1 1/2" baking dish. Heat 15 minutes at 350 degrees. Spoon into desert dishes; serve hot, warm, or cold.

*from THE DONOHO HOTEL COUNTRY KITCHEN COOKBOOK by Glenda Hill and Edith Walsh, Red Boiling Springs, Tennessee. Used by permission.

THE CORNER HOUSE
Cowan

Although six railroad charters were granted by the Tennessee Legislature in 1831, it was not until 1842 that the first train actually ran, and it made only a few trips before the company was taken over for debt. Owners of turnpikes and steamboats opposed the railroads, towns which might be bypassed feared the loss of trade, and people who invested in the few short-lived railroads lost their money.

In other states, railroads were succeeding; a line had been built from Charleston, South Carolina to the Savannah River opposite Augusta, Georgia, and as it approached Chattanooga by way of Atlanta, railroad fever began to rise again. Spurred by state aid, work began on the Nashville and Chattanooga Railroad in 1848, and although a tunnel through Sewanee Mountain was believed impossible, it was completed February 21, 1851.

This engineering feat was accomplished by two years of drilling from both sides, and down from the top, with only hand drills and black powder to cut through the solid rock. When the two ends met, there was great rejoicing. Hundreds of people marched through the tunnel with lighted candles, and that night there was a ball in Winchester. The tunnel was 2,228 feet long, and the track leading to it was the steepest grade railroad in the world.

At the base of the mountain, a depot was built in the little community of Cowan in 1852, and the town grew around the railroad.

When the Elk River Valley was settled after the War of 1812, among the earliest settlers were the Miller family. Farmers and later merchants, they contributed to the success of the town, and one of the Millers built a simple Queen Anne-style cottage in Cowan around the turn of the century.

With its low porch and cutaway bay window, the house had a comfortable, homey appearance that appealed to sisters Bobbye Cox and Freida Money. They bought it, decorated it appropriately with small-patterned wallpapers in dark green and rose, trimmed in crisp white, and in 1984 opened it as "The Corner House."

Here they serve what they modestly term "just home cooking." If so, it is the kind most people wish they had in their homes. An excellent Chicken Salad and Chicken Divan are always on the menu, but seasonal changes and new recipes may result in a creamy cheese soup with bits of pimiento and ham, or chewy orange spice muffins with raisins and orange peel, or perhaps a rum cake dripping with brown sugar, nut, and cherry glaze.

Whatever is available, it'll be freshly made of the freshest ingredients, and it won't be quite like anything you've tasted before.

"We work on recipes," Bobbye said, "maybe that we've used before, or that people have been nice enough to share with us. We do this, that, and the other to them to make them ours."

Their creative approach to home cooking is worth a trip across the mountain any time!

The Corner House, U.S. 64/41A, Cowan, is about 90 miles south of Nashville, about 12 miles off I-24. It is open for lunch 11 a.m. to 2 p.m., Monday through Saturday. (615)967-3910. Dress is casual, although most men wear jackets, and reservations are accepted. It is closed the week between Christmas and New Year's Day, and the busiest time is parents' weekend at The University of the South (Sewanee), the 3rd weekend in October. No credit cards are accepted, although personal checks are. ($$)

CORNER HOUSE LUNCHEON SHRIMP SALAD

2 pounds boiled shrimp,
  peeled and deveined
2 cups chopped celery
1 cup mayonnaise
3 teaspoons lemon juice

1 teaspoon dried
  dillweed
1 teaspoon salt
1/2 teaspoon pepper

Toss all ingredients and chill. Serve on lettuce with fresh tomato wedges.

CORNER HOUSE WHITE GAZPACHO

3 medium cucumbers,
  peeled and chunked
3 cups chicken broth
3 cups sour cream

3 Tablespoons vinegar
2 teaspoons garlic salt
Toppings (below)

Whirl cucumber chunks in blender with a little broth; combine with other ingredients just enough to mix. Chill. To serve, spoon into dishes and sprinkle with toppings.

Toppings : 2 tomatoes, peeled and chopped, 3/4 cup toasted almonds, 1/2 cup sliced green onions, 1/2 cup chopped parsley.

CORNER HOUSE FROZEN FRUIT SALAD

1 teaspoon gelatin
1 Tablespoon lemon
  juice
3 ounces cream cheese,
  softened
1/4 cup mayonnaise
1/4 teaspoon salt
2 Tablespoons powdered
  sugar

2 cups Cool Whip
1/4 cup chopped nuts
1/4 cup chopped
  maraschino cherries
16 ounces crushed
  pineapple
One 15-ounce can fruit
  salad

Soften gelatin in lemon juice. Mix all ingredients well, and freeze in paper baking cups.

CORNER HOUSE COLD OVEN POUND CAKE

1/2 cup margarine
1 cup Crisco
3 cups sugar
5 eggs
3 cups cake flour, sifted
  3 times

1 cup milk
1 teaspoon vanilla
1 teaspoon almond
  flavoring
Pinch of salt

Cream margarine and Crisco, gradually add sugar, then eggs, one at a time. Add milk and flour alternately, then flavorings. Beat at low speed. Pour in greased tube pan; start in cold oven, set at 325 degrees, and bake 1 hour 15 to 30 minutes.

HUNDRED OAKS CASTLE
Winchester

$\mathbf{A}$lbert S. Marks, a Kentuckian, relocated to Winchester, Tennessee in the late 1850s, where he married and set up a law practice. In the Confederate Army, he reached the rank of Colonel before losing a leg at the battle of Murfreesboro; he returned to Winchester, where he bought a large, two-story brick house outside town later called Hundred Oaks.

He was elected twenty-first Governor of Tennessee in 1878, but refused a second term due to the legislative dispute over railroad bond debts.

Marks' elder son, Arthur, traveled extensively during his years at the American Embassy in London. He met and married wealthy Mary Hunt, of Nashville, in 1888, and they returned to Hundred Oaks, where he immediately began an ambitious and romantic remodeling of the family home.

Marks' early writings describe his enthusiasm for the aged buildings in Europe, and with the assistance of Samuel M. Patton, a Chattanooga architect, he began changing the farmhouse into a Gothic Revival castle. A room similar to Sir Walter Scott's study at Abbotsford and an oak-paneled dining room were two realized fantasies among thirty-seven rooms. Embellished with a tower, dormers with dunce caps, and arched loggias, all executed by local artisans in local brick and ashlar, the house was never completed.

Governor Marks died in 1891, leaving his estate in trust to his grandson and namesake; Arthur Marks, having exhausted his wife's fortune, died in September, 1892. A year later his young widow remarried, and the property passed out of the family in 1899.

Catholic Paulist Fathers purchased and partially completed the house, using it as a monastery from 1901 to 1955. The barrel-vaulted hall became a chapel, and the paneled dining room was their refectory.

Numerous owners of the house and its diminished acreage came and went over the next twenty years; it often stood vacant. In the early 1970s, it was restored and used as a residence, then a restaurant and antique mall.

Believed to be one of 14 castles remaining in the United States,

Hundred Oaks Castle was placed on the National Register in 1975.

In 1985, the Castle and five acres were donated to the Franklin County Adult Activity Center, a non-profit community-based organization for retarded adults. Here, twenty-nine developmentally disabled clients are given useful training and work for which they are paid; at least twenty are involved with the restaurant.

Chef Louise Taylor supervises the kitchen staff, and describes her food as "Southern, home cooking, country fare." Everything is made from scratch, using mostly fresh products. On the buffet, you might find cheese or vegetable soup, fried chicken, ham with raisin sauce, or chopped steak with mushroom gravy, accompanied by REAL mashed potatoes, green beans almondine, scalloped potatoes, or the favorite candied yams with spices, fruits, and pecans.

Homemade breads include refrigerator rolls, banana bread, and assorted muffins (try pineapple!) with desserts of fruit cobblers, French coconut pie, and double fudge pie, all with crisp, flaky, homemade crusts.

It's not every day you can eat in a castle; in this one, you can feast like a king.

Hundred Oaks Castle is on US 64, 1/2 mile west of the town square. It is open for lunch Tuesday through Sunday, 11 a.m. to 2 p.m. From April through December, there is a menu and buffet lunch, and tours of the building are offered 9 a.m. to 3 p.m. January through March, there is only menu service, with buffet on Sunday, and tours are not available. It is closed the week between Christmas and New Year's Day. (615)967-0100. Dress is casual, and no credit cards are accepted, although personal checks are. ($)

HUNDRED OAKS BACON AND CHEESE SOUP

1/4 pound bacon	1/4 teaspoon thyme
1/4 cup flour	1/4 teaspoon
1 teaspoon paprika	Worcestershire
1 small onion, chopped	Pinch of garlic powder
2 1/2 cups milk, heated	Salt and pepper

1 pound cheddar cheese
1/2 cup grated parmesan cheese

Additional milk
Chopped parsley for garnish

Brown bacon until crisp; drain fat into saucepan, and stir in flour. Add paprika and onion, stir for 5 minutes, then stir in milk, cheese, and other spices, thinning with additional milk. Simmer 15 minutes, stirring frequently to avoid sticking. Crumble in bacon, and garnish with parsley.

HUNDRED OAKS BANANA MUFFINS

1/2 cup margarine
1 cup sugar
2 Tablespoons vanilla
2 eggs
1 cup mashed bananas
2 cups flour
3/4 teaspoon baking powder

1/2 teaspoon salt
3/4 teaspoon baking soda
1/4 cup boiling water
1/2 cup chopped pecans

In large bowl, blend margarine with sugar; add vanilla. Stir in next 5 ingredients, then soda mixed with boiling water. Stir in pecans and mix well. Fill greased muffin tins 2/3 full, and bake at 375 degrees for 15 minutes.

HUNDRED OAKS FRENCH COCONUT PIE

One 8-inch unbaked pie crust
3 eggs, beaten
1/2 stick margarine
1 1/3 cups sugar
1 Tablespoon flour

Pinch of salt
1/3 cup buttermilk
1 teaspoon vinegar
One 3 1/2-ounce can coconut

Cream butter and sugar; add rest of ingredients, and pour into pie crust. Bake 45 minutes at 350 degrees; cool before serving.

THE STUFFED GOOSE
Tullahoma

In December of 1862, Confederate General Braxton Bragg's forces held the Nashville- Chattanooga Turnpike near the little town of Murfreesboro. Inexplicably, Bragg had abandoned his northern offensive after the battle at Perryville, Kentucky, and had retreated into Tennessee.

Union General William S. Rosecrans began to move south from Nashville late in December. At dawn on December 31, Bragg attacked on a frozen field at Stone's River; after two days of bloody fighting, both armies were essentially where they had begun, although each army had lost more than a fourth of its men.

Believing Union reinforcements at hand, Bragg moved out after dark on January third, camping at Tullahoma. Rosecrans had lost his supplies, and limped into Murfreesboro. The armies spent six months only thirty-six miles apart.

In late June, 1863, Rosecrans moved south, but instead of the battle Confederates expected near Tullahoma, he headed for Chattanooga; Bragg's army was forced to move, and on July 3, Tullahoma fell to Union forces.

On a quiet side street in Tullahoma, a sprawling, comfortable house spreads wide, welcoming porches; several times remodeled, it was the family home of F.I. and Myrtle Couser for fifty-nine years. During the World War II housing shortage, they rented out rooms to young couples.

The happy memories many people had of this house began multiplying in late 1984, when Faye Whitt bought it and opened The Stuffed Goose.

"I run this just like my kitchen at home," Mrs. Whitt said, and that family feeling extends throughout the restaurant. Original rose and green wallpaper in the left front room set the color scheme for five additional dining rooms— the house is larger than it seems— ranging from the masculine "Hunt Room" to the tiny, romantic "Engagement Room" for two.

Fresh flowers and delicate tablecloths enhance lunch, which reflects "whatever's fresh and in season," and always includes soup, salad, hearty sandwiches, quiche or crêpe of the day, and a daily special that might be the popular hot chicken casserole. Chicken salad comes with a huge plate of fresh fruits, and

Bernice's hot potato rolls are irresistible. Desserts include homemade pies (don't miss the chess!) and a rich, gooey, "Chocolate Lush" guaranteed to wreck your diet.

The Stuffed Goose is at 115 North Collins, Tullahoma, and may be reached from Exit 111 off I-24. In Tullahoma, turn right on TN 55 at the end of the viaduct, to the Jackson/Lincoln intersection. Turn left, then right on Collins at the bank. It is open 11 a.m. to 3 p.m., Monday through Friday, dress is "dressy casual," and reservations are accepted, preferred for 6 or more. Busiest time is summer, especially August. V, MC. ($)

THE STUFFED GOOSE
HOT CHICKEN CASSEROLE*

4 cups cooked chicken, cut into chunks
1 cup finely chopped celery
1 teaspoon finely chopped onion
1/2 cup mayonnaise
1/2 teaspoon dry mustard
1/2 teaspoon lemon pepper

Two 10 3/4 ounce cans cream of celery soup
3/4 cup water
2 cups cooked rice, cooked in chicken broth
1 Tablespoon lemon juice
1 1/2 cups grated medium sharp cheddar cheese

Mix all ingredients except cheese; blend thoroughly. Pour into 9" x 13" baking dish. Cover and bake at 325 degrees for 30 minutes. Top with grated cheese and bake, uncovered, 15 minutes. Serves 6.

STUFFED GOOSE BUTTERNUT SQUASH*

2 pounds butternut squash, cooked and mashed
3/4 cup sugar
1/2 teaspoon baking powder

1 stick margarine
2 Tablespoons flour
2 eggs
1/2 teaspoon vanilla
Dash of nutmeg

In large bowl, mix all ingredients well. Pour into greased baking dish and cook at 350 degrees until firm. Serves 8.

STUFFED GOOSE APRICOT SALAD*

One 6-ounce package
  apricot gelatin
1 envelope plain gelatin
Two 16-ounce cans
  apricots (reserve
  juice)

1 20-ounce can crushed
  pineapple (reserve
  juice)
1 pint sour cream
Whipped topping and
  mint leaf for garnish

Dissolve apricot gelatin in 3 cups hot juice from fruits. Dissolve plain gelatin in 1/2 cup hot water, and add. Mix with fruit and sour cream, and pour into 9" x 12" pan; chill. Serves 24.

STUFFED GOOSE TENNESSEE PUDDING*

1 cup nuts
1 cup dates
1 cup coconut
3 1/2 cups flour
2 cups sugar
2 sticks margarine

4 eggs
1/8 teaspoon salt
1 teaspoon soda
1/2 cup buttermilk
1 teaspoon vanilla
Orange sauce (below)

Dredge nuts, dates, and coconut in flour, remove and set aside. Cream margarine and sugar until fluffy. Add eggs one at a time, beating well. Add salt to flour. Dissolve soda in buttermilk and beat until it foams to measure one cup. Alternately add flour and buttermilk to sugar mixture. Add vanilla, and fold in nuts, dates, and coconut. Bake in greased and floured 9" tube pan or 14" x 10" pan. Bake for 65 to 75 minutes at 300 degrees. While cake is hot, pour orange sauce over. Serve with whipped cream.

For orange sauce: Heat 1 1/2 cups orange juice with 2/3 cup brown sugar until dissolved.

* from BILL OF FARE, A Cookbook by the Stuffed Goose of Tullahoma, Tennessee. Copyright © 1988 Faye B. Whitt, Tullahoma, Tennessee. Used by permission.

MISS MARY BOBO'S
BOARDING HOUSE
Lynchburg

Landholder Thomas Rountree laid out the town that would become Lynchburg about 1818. His cabin, on a choice lot with two springs, was later enlarged; in 1867, owner Dr. E.Y. Salmon built an imposing Greek Revival frame house adjoining the older structure.

Called "The Grand Central Hotel," the house was home to long-term residents such as teachers, single men, and Revenue Agents inspecting Jack Daniel's new distillery. Mrs. Salmon had a talent for hospitality, and her table was always filled.

When Dr. and Mrs. Salmon retired in 1908, young Mary Bobo and her husband, Jack, took over the hotel, purchasing it in 1914. They called it "The Bobo Hotel," but, as the food's reputation grew, it became "Miss Mary Bobo's Boarding House."

Miss Mary operated the boarding house until her death in 1983, at the age of 101. Some years earlier, she had stopped renting rooms, serving only the midday meal, and when the Jack Daniel Distillery re-opened the house after her death, the same policy was continued.

Today, Proprietress Lynne Tolley, Jack Daniel's great-great niece, serves Miss Mary's old-fashioned Southern food family style, and presides over one of the five big tables.

"It's the best job in the world," she said. "I get paid to eat here every day, and meeting the people is lots of fun."

Over dinner of fried chicken and another meat, perhaps pot roast or meat loaf, accompanied by six Southern vegetables, often grown in the garden behind the house, plus cornbread, biscuits, or hot rolls, the stiffest stranger unbends.

Lynne tells stories about Lynchburg's past, explains unfamiliar foods to those from distant parts, and draws amusing anecdotes from guests. Hostesses at other tables, including Lynne's mother, Margaret Tolley, are equally adept. By dessert—possibly fruit cobbler, strawberry shortcake, or burnt-sugar cake with caramel icing— guests have become friends, and plan to return as soon as possible.

You will, too.

Miss Mary Bobo's Boarding House is just off the Lynchburg Town Square, 70 miles south of Nashville and 90 miles west of Chattanooga. It is about 45 minutes from I-24. "Dinner" is served PROMPTLY at 1 p.m., by reservation only. (615)759-7394. Dress is casual. MC, V, personal checks. ($$)

MISS MARY BOBO'S TIPSY SWEET POTATOES*

4 large sweet potatoes or
  yams
1/4 cup butter or
  margarine, softened
3/4 cup sugar

1/8 teaspoon salt
1/4 cup Jack Daniel's
  whiskey
1/2 cup pecans, coarsely
  chopped

In large saucepan, place potatoes with enough water to cover completely. Bring water to boil, cover, and cook potatoes about 35 minutes, or until tender. Drain, and when cool, peel.

In large mixing bowl, mash potatoes with next 4 ingredients and beat well. Spread 1/2 the mixture in a greased 1 1/2 quart round casserole and sprinkle with 1/2 the pecans. Repeat layers. Bake at 325 degrees about 30 minutes, or until pecans turn light brown. Serves 6 to 8.

MISS MARY BOBO'S
LADIES OF LYNCHBURG TEA LOAF*

3 cups flour
1 cup sugar
4 teaspoons baking
  powder
1 1/2 teaspoons salt
1/4 cup butter
2 teaspoons grated
  orange rind

1 1/2 cups chopped
  pecans
1 egg
1 cup milk
1/2 cup Jack Daniel's
  whiskey
1/4 cup chopped pecan

In bowl (or food processor), combine first 4 ingredients, and cut in butter until coarse crumbs. Stir in orange rind and pecans. In small bowl, mix liquid ingredients, and stir into flour mixture just until blended. Turn into greased and floured 9" x 5" x 3" loaf pan and sprinkle pecans over top. Bake about an hour, or until toothpick comes out clean. Cool in pan 10 minutes; turn onto rack to cool completely.

MISS MARY'S CABBAGE CASSEROLE*

1/2 small head of
　cabbage, chopped
1 small onion, chopped
1/2 green pepper,
　chopped
3 Tablespoons butter or
　margarine

3 Tablespoons flour
1 cup milk
1/2 cup shredded
　cheddar cheese
Seasoned cornbread
　crumbs

In saucepan, cook first 3 ingredients in lightly salted water until tender. Drain. In another saucepan, melt butter, stir in flour, and cook 1 minute, stirring. Add milk slowly and stir until thickened. Add cheese and blend until melted. Layer drained cabbage mixture and cheese sauce in greased casserole, ending with cheese sauce. Bake at 325 degrees until bubbly; top with crumbs and return to oven until lightly browned.

MISS MARY BOBO'S
TENNESSEE BARBECUE SAUCE*

1 medium onion, finely
　chopped
1 clove garlic, minced
2 Tablespoons vegetable
　oil
1 1/2 cups catsup
1/4 cup brown sugar
1 teaspoon liquid smoke

2 Tablespoons Jack
　Daniel's whiskey
2 1/2 Tablespoons cider
　vinegar
1/2 teaspoon dry
　mustard
2 drops hot pepper
　sauce

Sauté onion and garlic in vegetable oil until tender. Stir in remaining ingredients and bring to a boil over medium heat. Reduce heat and simmer for 10 minutes. Yields 2 cups.

*from Jack Daniel's THE SPIRIT OF TENNESSEE, Copyright © 1988 Lynne Tolley, Nashville, Tennessee. Used by permission.

THE TENNESSEE
WALKING HORSE HOTEL
Wartrace

Two means of transportation contributed to the town of Wartrace: the railroad and the horse.

Wartrace (or War Trail) Creek flowed through hunting lands frequented by Indians and early settlers. Used as a watering stop on the Nashville and Chattanooga Railway, it developed into a depot town when a rail spur was extended to Shelbyville, and was incorporated in 1903.

In 1917, Jesse Robert Overall and his wife, Nora, bought a lot on the railroad across from the commercial row of Wartrace, and built a three-story brick hotel, with verandahs overlooking the track. Catering to railroad workers, travelers, and salesmen, the hotel was also home to permanent residents.

About 1930, the Overall Hotel was sold to horse trainer Floyd Carothers and his wife Olive, who renamed it "Floyd's Walking Horse Hotel."

The Tennessee Walking Horse breed, first organized in 1935, is characterized by a "running walk" gait, in which the hind foot oversteps the print of the fore foot by several inches, producing a rapid, gliding, comfortable ride. On the ring he built behind the hotel, Mr. Carothers trained Strolling Jim, the first Tennessee Walking Horse World Grand Champion. Both lived out their lives there, and Strolling Jim is buried in a nearby meadow.

The hotel became an important gathering place for owners and trainers of the breed, but passed out of the Carothers family in 1958. It was being used as a home for veterans and was scheduled for demolition when it was purchased in 1980 by George Wright, who reestablished the name and set about its restoration. It was placed on the National Register in 1984.

The warm, welcoming atmosphere and comfortable rusticity of the hotel recall a simpler time, and guests relax on the verandah or watch horse show tapes in the lobby. Pictures of famous walking horses and their riders are in halls and the 25 guest rooms; George Wright hopes to make the hotel a center of information about the breed.

The dining room, just off the lobby, is the scene of fine traditional Tennessee meals; Tennessee country ham, creamed chicken over cornbread, and hot open-faced roast beef sandwich are lunch favorites, plus char-broiled rib eye and New York strip steaks and a "country gourmet" dish at dinner.

There's always a special of the day, and great country vegetables: squash casserole, green beans, fried apples, etc., with honey wheat bread and potato rolls made on the premises. If you have room for dessert, don't miss the Running-Walking cake, a prune spice cake with a yummy caramel glaze.

The Walking Horse Hotel, Wartrace, is seven miles from Shelbyville. Take exit 97 off I-24 to TN 64. It is open for breakfast 7:30 to 10:30 a.m., and lunch (Sunday dinner) 11:30 a.m. to 2:30 p.m., 7 days. Dinner is 5:30 to 9 p.m. Monday through Saturday. (615)389-6407. The hotel and restaurant are usually closed Monday through Thursday during the months of January and February. Dress is casual, and reservations are highly recommended. Busiest time is the 10-day Walking Horse Celebration, which ends the Saturday before Labor Day. MC, V. ($$)

WALKING HORSE HOTEL
CHEEZY BAKED BREAST OF CHICKEN*

For each serving:
1 chicken breast, skinned
Salt and pepper

Melted butter
1/4 cup crushed Cheez-It crackers

Season chicken, dip in melted butter, then roll in cracker crumbs. Bake at 350 degrees 45 minutes, basting with melted butter as needed.

WALKING HORSE HOTEL SQUASH CASSEROLE*

Crust:
1 stick margarine, melted

1 package Pepperidge Farm Herb Dressing Mix

Mix together thoroughly. Press half of mixture in 9" x 12" baking dish to form crust. Set aside.

1 1/2 pounds squash, cooked and drained

1 10-ounce can cream of chicken soup, undiluted

1 carrot, grated
1 medium onion, minced
One 2-ounce jar
   pimiento

8 ounces sour cream OR
2 heaping Tablespoons
   mayonnaise

Mix all ingredients and spread on crust. Sprinkle remaining crumbs on top. Bake at 350 degrees 45 minutes, until golden brown. Serves 10 to 12.

WALKING HORSE HOTEL
RUNNING-WALKING CAKE*

3 eggs
1 cup oil
1 1/2 cups sugar
2 cups flour
1 teaspoon soda
1/2 teaspoon salt
1 teaspoon cinnamon

1 teaspoon nutmeg
1 teaspoon cloves
1 cup buttermilk
1 cup chopped prunes
1/2 cup chopped nuts
Glaze (below)

In large bowl, blend eggs thoroughly with oil and sugar. Combine all dry ingredients, and add, alternating with buttermilk, to egg mixture. Stir in prunes and nuts. Pour into 9" x 13" baking pan, and bake at 350 degrees 35 minutes, until set. Pierce holes in top of cake and cover with glaze while still warm. Serve with a dollop of whipped cream, if desired.

For glaze: In large saucepan, mix 1 cup sugar, 1/2 cup butter or margarine, 1/2 teaspoon soda, 1/2 cup buttermilk, and 1 Tablespoon white corn syrup. Cook over low heat seven minutes, or until syrup turns golden.

*from TENNESSEE WALKING HORSE HOTEL STORYBOOK & COOKBOOK. Used by permission.

MÈRE BULLES
Nashville

The little settlement of Nashborough, clustered on a bluff overlooking the Cumberland River, was the center of seven forts under the Cumberland Compact. As the community grew, the name "Nashville" was used to include all seven sites, and the city was chartered in 1806.

Market Street, just a block from the original fort, was the focus of business activity from the first, growing in importance with the coming of steamboat traffic. In the 1870s and '80s, large commercial structures were built on the east side of Market Street utilizing the full width of the block, with access to river wharves on one side, and the street on the other, a full story higher.

Constructed during a period of highly individual architecture, many of these buildings have striking Italianate cornices and window designs; as a contiguous group, they constitute one of the best-preserved examples of Victorian commercial architecture in the country.

Market Street became Second Avenue in 1904; the Second Avenue Commercial District was placed on the National Register in 1972.

The largest and most elaborate of the structures, with three stories above street level, each with twelve arched windows, was built about 1872, and was first occupied by a carriage maker and a wholesale liquor distributor. Later, as a wholesale grocery company, it housed Joel Owsley Cheek, who developed the first commercially blended coffee.

Prior to his blend, most people purchased green coffee beans which they roasted and ground at home. By combining several different types of beans, and roasting and grinding them in bulk, Cheek produced a superior, consistent flavor. About 1892, he convinced the famous Maxwell House Hotel to serve his coffee, which he named for the hotel. President Theodore Roosevelt is credited with the praise that resulted in the "Good to the last drop" slogan.

Although the building subsequently housed other enterprises, it seems fitting that part of it is used once again for foods, beverages, and spirits. In 1987, a portion of the first floor became Mère Bulles (pronounced mare-bulls), a restaurant and wine bar. Its unusual name, a French translation of "Mother

Bubbles" resulted from a remark made by the owner's young grandson, who associated his grandmother with Champagne.

There is certainly Champagne at Mère Bulles, and a Cruvinet system provides many fine wines by the glass, but equally interesting and challenging is what marketing director Marion Wise terms a "California-type menu with a Continental flair."

Chef Chris Newton's entrées, frequently prepared in or sauced with wine, fit the romantic mood of the high-ceilinged brick dining rooms, where tall arched windows overlook the Cumberland, and open fires warm a winter night.

You might begin with a delicate Shrimp and Artichoke Bisque, and go on to Grilled Baby Salmon in a dill sauce, or Champagne Chicken. Lunches are light, with soups, salads, and sandwiches, plus hot entrées, and a group of daily specials that always includes a "Fitness Cuisine" special. Desserts, presented on a tray, are temptations; a favorite, called "Death by Chocolate," needs no explanation!

In the lounge, there's a separate menu of appetizers and interesting tastes— Tenderloin Tartare, with capers and onions, Grilled Raspberry Chicken, and Giant Sea Scallops in red pepper vinaigrette— that is available at all hours, and changes frequently.

Mère Bulles, 152 Second Avenue, N., Nashville, is open for lunch 11 a.m. to 2 p.m., Monday through Friday, for dinner 5:30 to 10 p.m. Monday through Thursday, to 11 p.m. Friday and Saturday; light foods are available between meals. Sunday brunch is 11 a.m. to 3 p.m. (615)256-1946. All beverages are served, including 50 wines by the glass, dress is "casually comfortable," and reservations are highly recommended, especially on weekends when they are sometimes made a week in advance. AE, DC, MC, V. ($$)

MÈRE BULLES
RASPBERRY VINAIGRETTE DRESSING

1 cup raspberries
1/2 cup extra virgin olive oil
1/4 cup raspberry vinegar

1 clove garlic, chopped
2 Tablespoons sugar
Basil, thyme, salt, white pepper

In blender, purée raspberries, slowly adding oil and vinegar, then spices to taste. Refrigerate overnight.

MÈRE BULLES BASIL CHICKEN ROTINI

1/2 pound rotini noodles, cooked al dente
Butter for sautéing
1 whole chicken breast, in julienne
1 plum tomato, diced

1 ounce dry white wine
Basil, salt, and pepper
1/3 cup grated parmesan cheese
1/3 cup heavy cream

In heavy skillet, melt butter and sauté chicken until almost done. Add tomato, wine and seasonings, and reduce by one half. Add cheese and cream, and cook until chicken is tender. Serve over noodles; serves 3 or 4.

MÈRE BULLES SEAFOOD JARDINAIRE

For each serving:
1 carrot, shredded
1 small yellow squash, in julienne
1 egg
Basil, salt, pepper, crushed garlic

White wine
Lemon juice
1 filet grouper or other white fish

In mixing bowl, mix first 6 ingredients to a thick paste. Lay filet flat and pack ingredients on top. Bake at 350 degrees about 20 minutes or until well browned.

THE MERCHANTS
Nashville

$\mathbf{B}$y 1860, Nashville was a bustling city of nearly 17,000 people, and Broad Street (later Broadway) extended from the wharf through a prosperous business and residential section.

On the corner of Cherry Street (later Fourth Avenue), a wholesale drug business was established in a three-story building, with a retail pharmacy on the first floor. The building was doubled in size in 1892, to become the Merchants Hotel, serving Nashville's business community.

The drugstore continued on the corner, with the hotel lobby next door; in addition to commercial travelers, the hotel sheltered vaudeville and early country music performers.

As commerce shifted to the suburbs, Broadway declined. Many buildings stood empty, threatened with demolition; others housed small businesses, taverns, and adult bookstores. Although some facades were altered, the importance of the area was recognized, and as part of the Broadway Historic District, the Merchants Hotel was placed on the National Register in 1980.

Nashville businessman Edward R. Stollman, instrumental in the restoration of Franklin, Tennessee, and active in Nashville's arts community, purchased the Merchants Hotel in 1983. Committed to reclamation of the building and the area, he also restored a former pawn shop adjacent to the hotel as a new home for the Metropolitan Arts Commission.

The exterior of the hotel was painstakingly restored, and the interior renovated to create The Merchants, a three-story American Grill, which opened in April, 1988. Filled with light, the first-floor Bistro has paneled walls, a horseshoe-shaped copper bar, and a lunch menu of soups, creative salads, and hearty sandwiches, with "Small Plates" appetizers available after five p.m.

More elaborate meals are served upstairs, where exposed brick walls sport an old sign for Ayres Sarsaparilla, and tall windows, curtained in lace, alternate with fireplaces. Here, in addition to downstairs choices, entrées include Grilled Salmon, wrapped in bacon and pepper with mustard dill butter; Five Pepper Chicken on linguine; and Blackened Snapper. Most, such as Arkansas Traveler (grilled marinated brisket with blackeyed peas and jalapeño corn bread) bow toward regional foods.

Desserts range from simple ice creams to a Chocolate Chip Hazelnut Bar with butterscotch sauce, and Butter Pecan Cheesecake oozing caramel and topped with a warm bourbon sauce.

Under the management of Dallas-based Dakota's Restaurants, the Merchants aims for the highest quality. "We bake all our own breads," said Operations Manager Jeff Barker. "We squeeze all juices, make all desserts and pastas, grill over native maple and hickory, and fly our own fresh fish in from Florida."

It shows. Already successful, The Merchants may boost a revitalization of the entire historic district.

The Merchants, 401 Broadway, Nashville, is entered from the side courtyard, and offers free valet parking in a secured lot. Lunch is 11 a.m. to 3 p.m., dinner from 5 to 10 p.m. weekdays, until 11:30 on weekends, with bar menu available between meals. (615)254-1892. Dress is casual, although most men wear coats and ties, all beverages are served, and reservations are highly recommended, almost a necessity on weekends. AE, CB, DC, MC, V. Bistro ($) Upstairs ($$$).

THE MERCHANTS CRAB CAKES

For each serving:

6 ounces jumbo lump crab

1/4 teaspoon finely minced serrano chili pepper

3/4 teaspoon finely chopped celery

1 1/2 teaspoons finely chopped purple onion

1 egg yolk

1/4 ounce semolina

3 drops Tabasco

1/2 teaspoon Worcestershire

Flour for dredging

1 egg, mixed with 1 tablespoon cold water

Bread crumbs

Oil for frying

Mix first eight ingredients. Form into 4 cakes, dredge in flour, dip in egg wash, then bread crumbs. Deep fry about 3 minutes, or until browned.

THE MERCHANTS MARINATED BRISKET

1 quart water
1 cup red wine vinegar
1 teaspoon cracked
  peppercorns
1 onion, chopped
4 bay leaves

2 teaspoons minced
  garlic
1 Tablespoon seasoning
  salt
1 beef brisket

Blend first seven ingredients. Trim excess fat from brisket, and soak overnight in marinade. Place brisket in baking pan, with just enough marinade to cover bottom. Cover with foil and bake about 1 1/2 hours at 350 degrees. Cool in its own juices. Slice when cool, then reheat to serve.

THE MERCHANTS GRILLED PORK CHOPS OVER GLAZED APPLES AND ONIONS WITH MAPLE PECAN BUTTER

Eight 5-ounce pork
  chops
Salt and pepper
Cooking oil
1 ounce butter
1 ounce brown sugar

2 red apples, cored,
  peeled, and sliced
4 ounces onion, in
  julienne
Maple Pecan Butter,
  (below)

Season and oil pork chops, and grill over medium heat, turning frequently. Heat butter in skillet. Add sugar, apples, and onion, and sauté until golden brown. To serve, divide apples onto four plates, top each with 2 chops, then ladle 1/4 of Maple Pecan Butter over top. Serves 4.

For Maple Pecan Butter: In skillet, sauté 1 teaspoon minced shallots in 1 Tablespoon butter. Add 2 ounces white wine and reduce by 1/2. Add 4 ounces cream, 4 ounces maple syrup, 1 1/2 teaspoons salt and 1/2 teaspoon white pepper and reduce by 1/2. Stir in 7 Tablespoons butter 1 at a time. Add 2 ounces toasted pecans just before serving.

THE HERMITAGE HOTEL
Nashville

For nearly fifty years after Tennessee became a state, the capital was wherever the Legislature voted to meet: Knoxville was capital three times; Kingston once, for one day; Nashville twice, and Murfreesboro once.

In 1843, when the Legislature finally made Nashville its permanent capital, the city purchased "Cedar Knob," the highest point in Nashville, for $30,000, and gave it to the state as a site for the Capitol.

As the seat of state government, coupled with its own flourishing economy, Nashville attracted numerous visitors, and many famous hostelries were built to accommodate them. Only the Hermitage Hotel remains, representing early twentieth-century grandeur at its pinnacle.

Opened in January 1910, the ten-story structure was designed in the Beaux-Arts style, which incorporates elements of several periods. It is impressive in its use of the finest materials and embellishments, with a two-story lobby beneath a stained glass skylight, and a ballroom panelled in walnut.

The Hermitage Hotel was placed on the National Register in 1975.

In its vaulted subterranean dining room, originally intended as a rathskeller, extraordinary food is served in an atmosphere of subdued elegance. American-Continental cuisine, under the direction of Executive Chef Karim Eskandari, is presented three times a day.

Breakfast offers a broad selection, with homemade pastries, waffles, and a "create your own omelet;" lunch provides appetizers, salads, sandwiches, and entrées such as Sautéed Brook Trout Meunière and Chicken Andalusia, plus a weekday buffet; and the Sunday Champagne Brunch menu is made up of favorite selections from other meals.

Dinner might include smoked salmon with dill sauce, French onion soup under a puff pastry crust, a salad of limestone lettuce with nuts and seafood, and quail stuffed with Italian sausage and drizzled with Hollandaise. Classic desserts, presented on a cart, range from Hermitage Mud Pie through Chocolate Mousse to luscious Crème Caramel, cut in a wedge and swimming in its own rich sauce.

The Hermitage Hotel, 231 Sixth Avenue, Nashville, has 112 overnight suites. (615) 244-3121. Breakfast is 6:30 to 10 a.m., to 10:30 weekends, lunch is 11 a.m. to 2 p.m., Sunday brunch is 11 a.m. to 2 p.m., and dinner is 6 to 10 p.m. weekdays and Sunday, to 11 p.m. on weekends. All beverages are served, daytime dress is casual, although most men wear coats and ties, which are required at dinner. Reservations are requested. AE, DC, MC, V. ($$$)

LOBSTER BISQUE À LA HERMITAGE

1/2 cup diced yellow onion
1/2 cup diced celery
2 cloves garlic, chopped
2 bay leaves
Two 1 1/2 pound live lobsters
1 quart water
10 ounces butter
3 teaspoons paprika
1 teaspoon lobster base, (optional)*

8 ounces flour
3 cloves garlic, chopped fine
1 quart whipping cream, heated
1 cup Sherry wine
Eight 4-inch squares puff pastry
1 egg, beaten with a little cold water

Place first six ingredients in heavy pan and boil about 15 minutes. Remove lobsters, cool and peel, chop and reserve, and keep stock warm. In saucepan, heat butter and add next four ingredients. Cook slowly until roux is well blended, then add to stock slowly, stirring until smooth. Bring to a boil. Add hot whipping cream, chopped lobster, and Sherry, and season to taste. Divide soup among eight 10-ounce soup bowls, top with pastry, and brush with egg wash. Bake at 400 degrees about 10 minutes, or until dough is done. Serves eight.

*Lobster base is a commercial preparation not readily available to the consumer.

HERMITAGE SALMON EN CROUTE
WITH LIME SAUCE

2 teaspoons fresh dill
  weed, chopped
Six 4-inch squares puff
  pastry
2 1/2 pounds fresh
  salmon, skinned and
  cut into six 6-ounce
  pieces
Salt and white pepper
Dill weed
10 fresh limes
6 raw jumbo shrimp
1 egg, beaten with a
  little cold water
Lime sauce (below)

Roll out dough, place salmon in center, shrimp on top, and sprinkle with salt, white pepper, and dill weed. Squeeze 1/2 lime on top of each, and wrap dough around salmon. Keeping seam on bottom, place salmon on oiled baking sheet. Brush with egg wash, and bake 20 to 25 minutes at 350 degrees, until dough is golden brown. Serve with lime sauce, with asparagus or broccoli and parsley new potatoes, garnished with lemon crown and sprig of fresh dill weed. Serves six.

For lime sauce: melt 8 ounces butter in saucepan, stir in 4 ounces flour, and cook for about 3 minutes, gradually adding 2 cups hot whipping cream and juice of seven limes. Cook ten minutes, and season with salt and pepper.

HERMITAGE KEY LIME MOUSSE

1 cup Rich's whipped
  topping
2 egg whites
1/2 cup powdered sugar
1/8 teaspoon yellow food
  coloring (optional)
Juice of 3 limes
1/3 cup bottled lime
  juice
2 ounces graham
  cracker crumbs
Whipped cream
Mint sprigs, and sliced
  limes for garnish

In large bowl, combine topping, egg whites, powdered sugar, and optional coloring. Whip until smooth, then add lime juices and crumbs. Whip about 3 minutes more; serve in champagne glasses, garnished with whipped cream, mint sprig, and sliced lime. Serves six.

THE UNION STATION HOTEL
Nashville

The Nashville and Chattanooga
Railroad was completed in 1854, the first long-distance railroad
in Tennessee. The Louisville and Nashville, in 1859, connected
Tennessee with traffic on the Ohio River.

Railroads, supremely important during the War Between the
States, were instrumental in rebuilding the South after the war.
In the 1870s, the Nashville and Chattanooga expanded to St.
Louis; controlling interests of the NC&St.L were purchased in
1880 by the L&N, which later absorbed the line.

Nashville railroad traffic was monopolized by the allied lines,
which were the cause of disgruntlement during the depression
of the 1880s. As employment increased with the Tennessee
Centennial Exposition, held a year late in 1897, spirits rose, and
the opening of the Union Station in 1900 was hailed as the
beginning of a new period of growth and prosperity for Nashville.

Fifty-seven acres in the city's eyesore "railroad gulch" had
been bought and cleared, and an enormous building in the
Richardsonian Romanesque style gradually took shape on Broad
Street. It was the first terminal designed by Richard Montfort,
later responsible for numerous L&N terminals.

Of Bowling Green stone and Tennessee marble, the Station is
characterized by arches, punctuated by soaring towers; its shed
was the largest unsupported span in the country, and could
house up to ten trains.

The main waiting room, with a barrel-vaulted stained-glass
skylight and bas-relief sculptures symbolizing Tennessee industry, was described as "altogether the most magnificent and
artistic... of any station in America."

As passenger travel declined, so did the Station; L&N offices
were relocated, and only a few trains passed through. Public
sentiment spurred campaigns to save it, and The Nashville
Union Station, placed on the National Register in 1969, was
named Tennessee's first National Historic Landmark in 1977.

Although the federal government became its owner in 1977,
little was done to rehabilitate the structure. In 1985, a group of
investors planned its conversion to a hotel complex, and renovation was accurate, thorough, and swift. Teams of workers first
removed accumulations of soot and dirt, then meticulously

restored stained glass, marble, and tile. Plumbing, wiring, and safety railings were brought up to code, and the magnificent Union Station Hotel opened late in 1986.

Today's visitor, awestruck by its grandeur and constant golden light, can hardly believe the years of neglect. Broadway's, in the glassed-in porch, provides three meals daily, with a generous breakfast selection; soups, salads, and sandwiches on the lunch menu are complemented by hot entrées and a buffet; and the Sunday brunch buffet covers most of the lobby and every wish of a hungry heart.

Dinner might begin with mushroom caps stuffed with crab meat, and proceed to Seafood Pasta Salad, and Steak and Shrimp Tempura, or Broiled Red Snapper Almondine. A selection of desserts includes pies, cakes, tortes, and always something unusual and exciting.

The Union Station Hotel is at 1001 Broadway, Nashville, and has 128 overnight suites. (615)726-1001. Food service, 7 days a week, includes breakfast, 6 to 10 a.m., lunch, 11 a.m. to 2:30 p.m., and dinner 5 to 11 p.m. Sunday brunch is 10:30 a.m. to 2:30 p.m. All beverages are served, dress is casual, and reservations are recommended. AE, DC, MC, V. ($$$)

UNION STATION HOTEL
BONELESS BREAST OF CHICKEN ROMANO

For each serving:

8 ounces boneless chicken breast

Romano marinade (below)

Flour for dusting

CLARIFIED butter for sautéing

1 ounce green pepper, in julienne

1 ounce sweet red pepper, in julienne

1 ounce sliced mushroom

Leeks sliced in rings

2 ounces white wine

Pinch of minced garlic

1/4 teaspoon minced shallot

Supreme sauce*

Salt and pepper

Marinate chicken breasts 48 hours. Remove from marinade, remove skins, wrap each breast separately, and refrigerate. To prepare, dust breast with flour, while CLARIFIED butter heats. Sauté chicken 2 to 3 minutes; turn and add peppers, mushrooms, leeks, and wine. Sauté on low heat. Add garlic and shallots and season. Finish with Supreme sauce.

For Romano Marinade for several uses, many chicken breasts: Mix together 1 quart oil, 2 quarts white wine, 6 bay leaves, 2 Tablespoons Rosemary, 1 Tablespoon oregano, 1 Tablespoon minced garlic, 1 Tablespoon basil, 2 Tablespoons salt, 1 teaspoon crushed red pepper, and one large onion, sliced. Refrigerate between uses.

*Most general cookbooks have a recipe for this classic sauce.

UNION STATION BAKED
STUFFED FILLET OF FLOUNDER

For each serving:

Two 6 to 8-ounce flounder fillets	**2 ounces CLARIFIED butter**
3 ounces crab meat stuffing (below)	**2 ounces white wine**

Cut flounder into 2-inch strips, tapering to the tail. With skin side up, distribute filling evenly over fillet. Roll tail end first, creating a spiral. Secure with pick. Place in pan, add butter and wine, and bake ten minutes at 500 degrees.

For crab meat stuffing: chop carrots, onion, and celery finely to total one cup. Sauté in CLARIFIED butter 3 to 5 minutes, stirring constantly. Add 1 1/2 Tablespoons sage, 1 teaspoon granulated garlic, 3 Tablespoons chopped parsley, and 1 1/2 cups crab meat, and sauté 5 minutes. Remove from heat and stir in 3 cups bread crumbs. Season to taste, moisten with heavy cream, let cool, and mix in 2 beaten eggs. Yields enough for six to eight servings.

CHEFS ON COMMAND
Nashville

Unsettled conditions in Germany in the 1830s drove thousands of Germans to emigrate. Among the first in Nashville were John and Mary Buddeke, whose impressive house on Seventh Avenue was used for Roman Catholic services. The center of German social life, a German community grew up around it.

The two-story brick commercial building behind it was built in 1884 by butcher Henry Neuhoff, later one of Nashville's prominent meat packers. When his success required more space, it became Fehr's Market, then Thompson's Drugs, and then only upstairs living quarters were occupied. As part of the Germantown Historic District, the building was placed on the National Register in 1979.

In 1983, Chefs on Command began their catering business in the rear of the store. Carry-out customers consistently carried their food only as far as the front room, however, and it was clear that a restaurant was needed.

Oak and walnut room dividers, patterned after mission-style hall trees, provide comfortable banquette seating in a spacious room filled with light. Woodwork and pressed-tin ceiling in dark green set off old wooden floors and antique tables; the feeling is one of relaxed charm.

Part-owner/ Chef Kevin Rule's attitude undoubtedly affects the atmosphere. He is comfortable and excited at the same time, aware that his food is something special. "I take a lot of pride in what I'm doing," he said.

At lunch, try his unusual gazpacho or rich gumbo, thick with shrimp and green peppers. Salads, such as the American, with chunks of fried chicken, tomato, and avocado, topped with shredded Swiss cheese and almonds, come with outstanding homemade dressings, and even a tuna sandwich is a wow: grilled tuna on an onion roll with a sauce of cucumbers and green onions.

Weekend dinners are more formal, but equally creative. White napery, Tiffany china and glassware, and European service ensure luxurious dining, and choices of four appetizers and five entrées make up a menu that changes quarterly. Each plate is a picture, and meals end with demitasse and Kevin's incredible desserts.

"I've spent a lot of time working with and studying chocolate," he said. As evidence: White Chocolate Cheesecake; Walnut Rhapsody (a flourless cake of walnuts and chocolate with rum chocolate buttercream); Black Velvet (sponge cake filled with chocolate mousse and glazed with chocolate); and there's even a chocolate bag, filled with white chocolate mousse and raspberry sauce....

Chefs on Command, 1239 Sixth Avenue North at Monroe, Nashville, may be reached from the Jefferson Street exit off I-65. Drive west to 4th, north to Monroe, and west to 6th. Lunch, Monday through Friday, is 10:30 a.m. to 2:30 p.m.; Prix fixe Dinner, by reservation only and limited to 30 people, is served Friday and Saturday from 6 to 10 p.m. (615)255-9583. Wines are served and dress is casual, but not TOO casual. Busiest time is during Germantown's Oktoberfest, and the restaurant is closed the first three weeks of the year. AE, MC, V. ($$) prix fixe ($$$)

CHEFS ON COMMAND
ROASTED RED PEPPER VINAIGRETTE

1 clove garlic, peeled
1/4 cup basil leaves
2 Tablespoons red wine vinegar
1 1/2 Tablespoons Dijon mustard
1/4 teaspoon dried rosemary
1 sweet red pepper, roasted
1/4 cup olive oil
Salt and pepper

Pulverize garlic in food processor; add basil and chop. Scrape bowl, then add remaining ingredients except olive oil. Process until smooth, then slowly add olive oil, and season.

CHEFS ON COMMAND LOBSTER SAUTÉ

One pound angel hair or other pasta
1/4 cup butter
1 1/2 cups cooked, chopped lobster meat
1/2 cup chopped green onion

152

1 Tablespoon lobster
  butter (optional,
  below)
1 sweet red pepper,
  diced
1 sweet yellow pepper,
  diced

1/2 teaspoon lemon zest
Sauvignon Blanc wine
4 Tablespoons sour
  cream
4 teaspoons black
  caviar, optional

Boil pasta according to directions on package. Drain. Melt butter in skillet with optional lobster butter. Sauté peppers one minute. Add lobster meat and stir to heat. Add green onion, lemon zest and wine, and pour sauté over pasta. Top each serving with one Tablespoon sour cream and one teaspoon caviar. Serves 4.

For Lobster Butter: Chop lobster shells into small pieces and sauté in 1/2 cup butter. Strain shells and reserve the lobster-flavored butter.

CHEFS ON COMMAND
AMARETTO BREAD PUDDING

3/4 cup raisins
8 cups broken bread
  pieces
2 cups half and half
  cream
2 cups heavy cream

3 eggs
1 1/2 cups sugar
1 Tablespoon almond
  extract
3/4 cup sliced almonds
Amaretto sauce (below)

Soak raisins overnight in amaretto to cover. Soak bread in cream and half and half for one hour. Mix eggs, sugar, and almond extract. When bread is soft, fold in egg mixture, drained raisins, and almonds, and pour into buttered 9" x 13" baking dish. Bake at 350 degrees 50 to 70 minutes, until top achieves desired crispness.

For Amaretto sauce: In top of double boiler, stir together 1/2 cup butter and one cup powdered sugar until very hot. Remove from heat and whisk in one egg, beaten, until mixture is room temperature, then add 4 Tablespoons amaretto.

THE STOCK YARD RESTAURANT
Nashville

Nashville's early market, near the courthouse, provided a sales location for farmers and small merchants, but few meat products were sold. Butchering was done primarily in November, or when cold weather insured against spoilage; meats were smoked, salted, or pickled, to aid in preservation.

German and Swiss immigrants, who settled in North Nashville in the 1840s, brought new products and techniques to increase shelf life in pre-refrigeration days. The famous Nashville Spiced Round of Beef, pierced with strips of pork fat rolled in spices, then cured in brine,was a Christmas delicacy enjoyed by Nashvillians of all backgrounds; boneless hams, first introduced at the Tennessee Centennial in 1897, were the beginning of lunchmeats in Nashville.

In 1898, the Abattoir Association brought together individual slaughtering operations, and in 1917, James Caldwell, Sr., was instrumental in forming the Nashville Union Stockyards.

A handsome L-shaped building in North Nashville was constructed in 1920, and housed various businesses related to the sale of stock, plus banks, barber shops, and a restaurant. There was even a Post Office and a Western Union office— livestock was big business, and the Nashville Union Stockyards was one of the most successful businesses of its kind in the Southeast.

The Stockyards closed in 1974, and in 1979, a group of Nashville businessmen, including country music executive Buddy Killen and restaurateur Mario Ferrari, renovated it into The Stock Yard Restaurant.

Primarily a steakhouse, the restaurant, now owned by Killen, serves hundreds of people daily in dozens of dining rooms. "We're trying to do everything as fresh as possible," said General Manager Eric Anderson, "except our beef, which is aged six weeks. That's part of our secret for having a filet three inches thick that you can cut with a fork."

Visible from the entrance hall, beef is stored in a windowed, climate-controlled room at about thirty-eight degrees, and after aging, is served in portion sizes that range from a six-ounce Filet Mignon to a twenty-two-ounce Porterhouse, cooked to your exact requirement. There are also chicken, seafood, pork, and combinations, and each dinner includes soup, salad, vegetable, and hot bread and butter.

Luncheon menu adds sandwiches and salads, and a "Home Cooked" menu that changes daily, and might be fried chicken, pork chops, or meat loaf, with country vegetables, corn cakes, and sliced tomatoes.

The Stock Yard's Hot Cheesecake is light and delicate, with dark chocolate sauce, or you might choose a huge wedge of gooey pecan pie, dutch apple pie, or an old-fashioned hot fudge sundae, before repairing to the Bull Pen Lounge for country music entertainment and a chance to look for famous faces in the audience. There are always at least a few.

The Stock Yard Restaurant, 901 Second Avenue, North, Nashville, provides off-street parking, or will send a free limousine to local hotels for parties of four or more. It is open for lunch Monday through Friday, from 11 a.m. to 2 p.m., and for dinner Monday through Saturday from 5 to 11 p.m. (615)255-6464. All beverages are served, dress is "nice casual," and reservations are required for parties of 8 or more. A waiting list begins at 7:30 every night; no reservations are taken for small parties. Busiest times are Vanderbilt home football games. AE, DC, MC, V, Discover. ($$$)

STOCK YARD BLUE CHEESE DRESSING

1 cup buttermilk
1 Tablespoon parsley
1 Tablespoon dried
chives
Dash garlic powder

1/4 teaspoon black
pepper (optional)
1/4 cup mayonnaise
1/4 pound blue cheese

Pour buttermilk in bowl of electric mixer and place mixer at slow speed. Add chives and parsley, garlic powder, optional pepper, and mayonnaise. Stop mixer and slowly fold in blue cheese. Caution: the more you mix, the smaller the chunks of cheese. Refrigerate.

JIMMY KELLY'S
Nashville

In the early days of Nashville, most homes were downtown, close to business and government. As the city grew, demands for business locations, plus crowded and unsanitary conditions, drove people to build new homes in the suburbs. Soon businessmen were working in the very areas in which they once had lived.

Restaurants which catered to businessmen flourished in the downtown area; one of these, the "216 Club," a father and son operation, opened in 1934. When a second location was required, the son, Jimmy Kelly, opened a restaurant on Harding Road under his own name in 1949. Popular steak houses, equally known for piping-hot, bite-sized corn cakes, the downtown location lasted until 1965, and the Harding Road restaurant until construction forced it to move in 1982.

The house they chose had an interesting background; built about 1911 for one of the founders of the National Life and Accident Insurance Company, it had later been home to the Ladies of Charity and to the Nashville Woman's Club. Used for social events and weddings, the gracefully proportioned Italian Renaissance-style house had an open, hospitable atmosphere that adapted well to restaurant use.

Owned by Jimmy Kelly's brother, Bill, and managed by Bill's son, Mike, Jimmy Kelly's is one of Nashville's most stable restaurant traditions. "We're known for our beef," Mike said, "and three years ago, when we decided we needed an alternative, we didn't want to put something second-rate on the menu. We were very fortunate; there are new purveyors and new methods of shipping fish, and our fish is flown in daily."

The daily special fish joins Midwestern beef, aged four to six weeks, minimum, and cut on the premises; grilled lamb and veal chops; blackened catfish; broiled half chicken; and Tennessee country ham steak for a simple but satisfying menu.

If you mention Jimmy Kelly's to anyone who has dined there, they immediately respond with "corn cakes!" The enthusiasm is unmistakable. About two inches in diameter, crusty and brown, yet puffy in the center, they are brought to the table as soon as guests are seated with an enormous plate of quite unnecessary butter. Imitated by many people— including some famous chefs— they remain a delicious secret.

Popular salads include an asparagus-tomato combination, and Faucon Salad (bacon, eggs, and lettuce with Roquefort dressing), and everyone tries to save room for such desserts as fried ice cream, with caramel walnut sauce; New York Cheesecake, Jack Daniel's Turtle Pecan Pie, and the aptly named Chocolate Suicide Cake.

Jimmy Kelly's, 217 Louise Avenue, Nashville, is at the corner of State Street, three blocks off West End. It is open for dinner only, Monday through Saturday, 5 p.m. to 12 Midnight; a limited menu "Late Supper" is served after 10:30 p.m. (615)329-4349. All beverages are served, dress is casual, and reservations are accepted. AE, DC, MC, V. ($$$)

JIMMY KELLY'S BLACKENED CATFISH

Six 8 to 10-ounce catfish filets
1 3/4 cups unsalted butter

Spice Mixture (below)
Lemon slices for garnish

Heat a large cast-iron skillet at least 10 minutes (the hotter the better). Melt butter in separate pan; reserve 3/4 cup butter to serve with fish. Dip filets in butter, coating both sides well. Sprinkle spice mixture evenly on both sides of fish. Cook over high heat until underside forms a crust. Turn and repeat. Serve with melted butter and slice of lemon. Serves 6.

Note: this cooking method produces intense smoke.

For Spice Mixture: In bowl, blend 1/4 cup EACH: red pepper, white pepper, and paprika, with 2 Tablespoons dry mustard, 2 Tablespoons fennel, 1 teaspoon cumin, and 1 teaspoon garlic powder.

JIMMY KELLY'S CHATEAUBRIAND

2 to 3 pounds beef
   tenderloin (8 ounces
   per person)
Freshly ground black
   pepper
Lawrey's Seasoned Salt

10 to 12 jumbo white
   mushrooms, sliced
2 1/2 cups Cabernet
   Sauvignon or other
   red wine, divided

Remove all fat from tenderloin; place flat on large broiling pan, and coat with pepper and seasoned salt. Place in preheated 450 degree oven on middle rack for 10 minutes, then add mushrooms and 1 cup wine. Cook 10 additional minutes for rare, 20 additional minutes for well done. Remove to warm serving plate. Deglaze pan with remaining red wine, and serve as sauce on the side.

A Jimmy Kelly's Note: Fresh vegetables such as asparagus, broccoli, and cauliflower are traditionally served with Chateaubriand.

MARIO'S RISTORANTE
Nashville

During the War Between the States, no Southern city, with the possible exception of New Orleans, suffered as Nashville did under Union occupation. A city of Southern sentiment in a divided state, Nashville was under martial law from February, 1862, until the end of the war.

Although retreating Confederates had burned bridges and any military equipment they could not carry, Federals seized warehouses and their remaining contents, and made Nashville a supply depot for the area between Cumberland Gap and the Mississippi River. Private dwellings were taken over to house troops, and larger structures, including churches, commercial buildings, and the State Capitol, were made into hospitals.

Citizens of Nashville had few rights; undisciplined soldiers and camp followers roamed the streets and took whatever they wanted, and while Federals were well supplied, civilians found it difficult to obtain necessities. Food, clothing, and medicine were horribly expensive and in short supply, and substitutes were made for items impossible to find. Ersatz coffee was made from acorns, sweet potatoes, or peanuts; cornbread replaced breadstuffs made from white flour; and molasses, itself scarce, was used in place of sugar, which had disappeared entirely.

After the war, Nashville eventually became the gracious, cultural city it had been, with new industry contributing to a population of nearly a hundred thousand by 1895. Growth to the west side of town had been slow, partly due to the railroad "gulch," but residential development increased toward Vanderbilt University.

A house built in the vicinity in the 1890s is now the core of one of Nashville's most popular restaurants. A conversion to apartments in the 1920s obscured the original facade, and the two major dining rooms are in what was once the front yard. With their high ceilings, they contribute to what owner/chef Mario Ferrari calls "the theatre of dining."

Subtle lighting, reflected in copper sheathing on the walls, creates an atmosphere that is the perfect background for superb Northern Italian cuisine. Flowers, candles, silver, and European service, plus a selection from Mario's 200,000-bottle wine collection, add up to a very special evening.

Try the Antipasto Assortito for a sampling of marvelous flavors, then a crisp salad, followed by poached salmon over sautéed spinach, or one of the outstanding veal dishes. You might just ask your captain to choose for you— you can't go wrong.

Desserts vary, but frequently include Zuppa Inglese (liqueur-soaked sponge cake with custard and cream); Grasshopper Cheesecake; Chocolate Cake with espresso icing; and Tira Misu, a cheesecake-like custard over sponge cake soaked in espresso, topped with whipped cream.

Mario's Ristorante, 2005 Broadway, Nashville, is open for dinner Monday through Saturday, 5 to 11 p.m. (615)327-3232. All beverages are served, including an extensive wine collection, dress requires a jacket for men, and reservations are strongly advised. The restaurant is closed the week between Christmas and New Year's. AE, DC, MC, V. ($$$)

MARIO'S FETTUCCINE GORGONZOLA*

4 large shallots, chopped
1/4 cup butter
3/4 cup crumbled
  gorgonzola
1/2 cup cherry tomato
  wedges
1/2 cup slivered
  prosciutto
1/4 teaspoon salt
1/8 teaspoon pepper
2 Tablespoons light
  cream
One 8-ounce package
  fettuccine, cooked
2 Tablespoons chopped
  parsley

In skillet, sauté shallots in butter until tender. Add next 5 ingredients; toss lightly. Stir in cream. Combine with hot fettuccine in hot serving dish; toss lightly. Garnish with parsley and serve immediately. Serves 6 to 8.

MARIO'S SCAMPI TRIESTE*

3 cloves garlic, minced
2 Tablespoons olive oil
2 Tablespoons butter
1 1/2 pounds shelled,
1/4 cup minced fresh
  parsley
6 Tablespoons bread
  crumbs

deveined shrimp

1 cup dry white wine

1/4 cup lemon juice

1/2 cup chopped
scallions

1 Tablespoon capers

1/2 teaspoon salt

1/4 teaspoon pepper

In skillet, sauté garlic in mixture of olive oil and butter without browning. Add shrimp and cook 3 to 6 minutes, or until just firm. Place shrimp on heated platter; keep warm. Add wine to skillet, stirring to deglaze; reduce to about 1/3 cup. Add lemon juice and cook until liquid is almost evaporated. Add scallions, parsley, and shrimp. Sprinkle bread crumbs, capers, and seasonings over shrimp; toss to mix well. Broil for 1 minute and serve immediately. Serves 4.

MARIO'S PAGLIA E FIENO (STRAW AND HAY)*

1 cup heavy cream

2 cups cooked peas

1 cup chopped
prosciutto OR
smoked ham

1/2 cup grated parmesan
cheese

1/4 teaspoon salt

1/2 teaspoon pepper

6 ounces fettuccine

6 ounces green
fettuccine

In saucepan, heat cream without boiling. Stir in next 5 ingredients and cook for five minutes, or until heated through, stirring occasionally. Cook fettuccine al dente; place on heated serving platter. Pour sauce over fettuccine; toss gently. Garnish with additional parmesan cheese. Serve immediately. Serves 4.

* from MARIO FERRARI ON WINE AND FOOD, with Joan Dew. Copyright © 1985 Mario Ferrari, Nashville, Tennessee. Used by permission.

PEOPLES
of Carter's Court
Franklin

Ambitious Confederate General John B. Hood, frustrated after the Battle of Atlanta in the late summer of 1864, took his Army of Tennessee on a circuitous route to invade Tennessee. Unaware of Union strength, he planned to recapture Nashville and drive Federal forces back across the Ohio River.

With about 23,000 infantry, he joined General Nathan Bedford Forrest's cavalry at Tuscumbia, Alabama, and proceeded north to Spring Hill, Tennessee.

Union General John M. Schofield, sent to assist in the defense of Nashville, marched toward Columbia, Tennessee, on a parallel route. After a skirmish at the Duck River, Federals retreated, and on the night of November 29, overconfident Hood went into bivouac for the night at Spring Hill, while Schofield's entire force passed nearby.

Infuriated by his missed opportunity, Hood sent his men against firmly entrenched Federals at Franklin the following day. In full view of their enemy, under artillery fire from two directions, Confederate forces charged repeatedly. Up the Columbia Pike and into fields around the Carter House, hand-to-hand fighting raged fierce and bloody; in about five hours, The Army of Tennessee was virtually destroyed.

A contemporary Confederate account reads: "Never in the history of any war did men rush into the jaws of death with more gallantry than at Franklin, and there we lost the veteran troops, the flower of our army, with 5 general officers killed and 7 wounded." The five Confederate generals killed at Franklin were laid on the porch at Carnton, and 1500 Confederates were buried in the family cemetery nearby.

About 1889, a school was built on the site of the battle. First called "Mooney School", for its first headmaster, it was renamed Battle Ground Academy. A later headmaster, R.H. Peoples, lived and rented rooms to students in a Victorian cottage built across the road about 1903.

His cottage became a tea room in 1974, anchor of a new minimall of shops and boutiques, and in October, 1987, it became Peoples of Carter's Court, a full-service restaurant known for gracious dining.

Its charming interior, bright and airy, with columned dividers separating rooms, is the scene of many excellent meals, guided by manager Rod Pewitt, and prepared by Rachel Jones and Chef Marty Cook. Luncheon soups, salads, and sandwiches are complemented by an old-fashioned Blue Plate Special, Spa Cuisine, and the Best of the Wurst, plus pasta, seafood, and quiche of the day.

You might begin your evening meal with Drunken Shrimp, and go on to Chicken Desmond, stuffed with blue crab, spinach, and Swiss cheese, and topped with rosemary Hollandaise, or Veal Anthony, sautéed with artichoke hearts, red wine, and mushrooms. Fresh fish, several pastas, and steaks round out a generous menu, and you can choose from an array of desserts, changed daily. Favorites include a gooey brownie, topped with ice cream and splashed with Kahlúa, peanut butter pie drizzled with chocolate, and New York cheesecake in a puddle of raspberry/brandy/caramel sauce.

Peoples of Carter's Court is at 1143 Columbia Avenue, Franklin, and is open 7 days for lunch, 11 a.m. to 2:30 p.m., and for dinner Tuesday through Thursday, 5:30 to 9 p.m., until 10 p.m. Friday and Saturday. (615)790-9075. Dress is casual, all beverages are served, and reservations are accepted, preferred for 5 or more. Busiest time is during December's Candlelight Tour of Homes and Dickens of a Christmas celebrations. AE, MC, V. ($$)

PEOPLES CRANBERRY CHICKEN

4 chicken breasts
Butter for sautéing
Flour for dredging
2 ounces white wine for
   deglazing pan

6 ounces canned whole
   cranberries
1 cup heavy cream
Salt and pepper

In skillet, sauté chicken breasts in butter about 5 minutes or until done. Add wine and deglaze pan, then add cranberries and cream and simmer about 5 minutes. Serves 4.

PEOPLES VEAL IMPERIAL

Eight 2-ounce veal
   scallops
Butter for sautéing

1 medium tomato, diced
Pinch of garlic
   (optional)

168

2 ounces hearts of palm, cut into small pieces
3 green onions, sliced

2 cups heavy cream
Salt and pepper

In skillet, sauté veal in butter about 1 minute on each side. Add vegetables, then cream and optional garlic. Simmer until cream is thick; season to taste. Serves 4.

PEOPLES RACHEL'S CREAMED CHICKEN

One whole chicken, boiled, deboned, and chopped
2 quarts reserved chicken broth
1 large onion, chopped

3 stalks celery, chopped
3 carrots, shredded
1/2 cup cornstarch
1 cup half and half cream
Salt and pepper

In large pan, cook chicken and vegetables in reserved broth until vegetables are done. Add cornstarch, mixed with a little of the broth, and cook until thickened. Add cream, season to taste, and serve over cornbread squares. Serves 10 to 12.

PEOPLES HOT SPICED LEMON-LIME DELIGHT

Tea, with water to make one gallon
1 3-ounce package lemon gelatin
1 3-ounce package lime gelatin

2 cinnamon sticks
Sugar, if desired
Slices of lime and lemon, for garnish

Brew a gallon of tea; add gelatin and cinnamon sticks to hot mixture and bring to a boil. Add sugar, if needed, to taste. Serves 18-20.

CHOICES
Franklin

The land grant of Anthony Sharp, a North Carolina soldier in the Revolution, was bought in 1787 by Abram Maury, who laid out a town. Incorporated in 1815, Franklin was, by mid-nineteenth century, the center of one of the most prosperous and beautiful areas in "The West," surrounded by impressive farm homes and sweeping, fertile fields.

The horrendous Battle of Franklin and its aftermath left the area physically damaged and economically impoverished, but it was soon producing crops from its rich earth. Without slave labor after the war, however, farmers turned chiefly to tobacco.

The town of Franklin continued to be a trading center for outlying farms; most of the commercial buildings surrounding and near the square were built toward the end of the nineteenth century.

In February of 1899, James W. Harrison bought the home of his mother-in-law on the corner of Fourth Avenue and Main Street, and demolished it to make way for a dignified two-story commercial building. Characterized by impressive brickwork, the Harrison Building was joined in 1902 by a duplicate structure, giving the appearance of one massive building.

The corner building, rented by Walter Bennett and occupied by Bennett and Campbell Hardware, was a favorite gathering place of people who came to town on Saturdays. Filled with plows, paint, tools and supplies, it became known as "Bennett's Corner." As part of the four-block Franklin Historic District, it was placed on the National Register October 5, 1972.

When it became a restaurant in the summer of 1984, the upstairs lounge (with its own recreated trolley car) retained the name "Bennett's Corner;" downstairs is a handsome multi-level restaurant called "Choices."

And your choices are many. The food, characterized as "Southern Gourmet," changes seasonally, but you can count on soups, salads, and sandwiches at lunch, as well as light entrées such as Vegetarian Pasta or Chicken-Mushroom Crêpes with sherry sauce.

The dinner menu adds appetizers and pastry-covered onion soup, with entrées "from the water, from the air, and from the land." Try the Sautéed Fresh Rainbow Trout with crab meat, or

171

the Chicken Manhattan, grilled with spinach, mushrooms, and cheese. Light suppers include burgers and marinated grilled chicken breast on a bun. For dessert, you might sample the delicate Cold Lemon Soufflé in its own sauce, or the signature Harpeth River Mud Pie: coffee ice cream and Kahlúa in a chocolate crumb crust, topped with whipped cream and dusted with cocoa.

Choices, 108 4th Avenue S. at Main Street, Franklin, is open Monday through Saturday for lunch, 11 a.m. to 2 p.m., and Monday through Thursday for dinner, 5:30 to 9 p.m., until 10 p.m. Friday and Saturday. Sunday breakfast is 9 to 11 a.m., and "Sunday Down South" buffet is 11 a.m. to 2 p.m. Bennett's Corner provides buffet lunch Monday through Friday, 11 a.m. to 2 p.m., with food service 4:30 to 11 p.m. (615)791-0001. Dress is casual, all beverages are served, and reservations are accepted for parties of five or more. Busiest time is during Dickens of a Christmas celebration, the middle two weeks of December. AE, MC, V. ($$)

CHOICES
CRANBERRY WALDORF CONGEALED SALAD

4 cups boiling water
Two 3-ounce packages
cherry gelatin
Two 3-ounce packages
strawberry gelatin
One 16-ounce can whole
cranberry sauce

1 can ice cubes
1 cup chopped English
walnuts
1 cup chopped, unpeeled
red apples

Dissolve gelatin in boiling water; add cranberry sauce and mix well, then stir in ice cubes and walnuts, finally apples. Pour into oblong dish that will hold 2 quarts and chill; cut into squares to serve.

CHOICES SPOON ROLLS

1 package dry yeast
2 Tablespoons water at
 110 degrees
2 cups warm water

3/4 cup vegetable oil
4 cups self-rising flour
1/4 cup sugar
1 egg, beaten

Dissolve yeast in 2 Tablespoons water; combine all ingredients well. Spoon into greased muffin tins and bake 15 to 20 minutes at 400 degrees. Batter will keep in refrigerator for several days.

CHOICES SAWDUST PIE

One 8-inch unbaked pie
 crust
1 1/2 cups graham
 cracker crumbs
1 1/2 cups coconut
1 1/2 cups chopped
 pecans

1 1/2 cups sugar
1 cup egg whites (about
 seven)
Whipped cream and
 sliced bananas for
 garnish

Mix all ingredients well. Pour into pie shell and bake 45 minutes at 350 degrees. Serve with whipped cream and sliced bananas.

MAGNOLIA HOUSE
Columbia

Maury (pronounced Murray) County was formed in 1807, and the seat was named for Christopher Columbus. Among the earliest settlers were surveyor Samuel Polk and his wife, Jane, who built a town house about 1816 while their son James was at the University of North Carolina.

James, an outstanding student, was graduated in 1818, returned home, was admitted to the bar, and married, intending a political life. A member of the Tennessee Legislature, a representative in Congress from 1825 to 1839, serving as Speaker the last four years, and Governor of Tennessee from 1839 to 1841, James K. Polk was eleventh President of the United States, from 1845 to 1849.

A hardworking and decisive leader, Polk demanded annexation of Texas and fixed the northwest boundary by treaty with Great Britain, opening the west for migration. His health was never good; exhausted by the strain of his responsibilities, he returned to Nashville after one term, and died in a cholera epidemic June 15, 1849.

Around the corner from the Polk home, a two-story frame house was built for Dr. D.N. Samson before 1820, in a neighborhood called "Quality Hill." It was extensively remodeled about 1850 by Nathan Vaught, a distinguished local master builder; many houses he built and remodeled during the period have similar interior elements. The graceful one-story Gothic-revival porch was probably added at that time.

Known as the "Doctors' House" for the succession of physicians who occupied it, it was placed on the National Register in 1978, as part of the West Sixth Street and Mayes Place Historic District.

In 1981, it became a restaurant, and now serves interesting lunches in a gentle Southern atmosphere. There's a grandmotherly feeling about the Magnolia House; dignified, yet welcoming, the wide double parlor in peach and cream now serves as main dining room, and the fragrance of hot rolls is everywhere.

There's an all-you-can-eat lunch buffet on Wednesday, Thursday, and Sunday, offering four salads, three meats, three vegetables, two breads, and three desserts, and the menu is equally generous.

Salads, sandwiches, burgers and dogs join quiche of the day, creamed turkey on eggbread, and hot entrées to provide something for everyone, with homemade pies such as chocolate, lemon ice box, coconut, and a marvelously dense, chewy peanut butter.

Magnolia House, 701 N. High Street, Columbia, is on the corner of Sixth Street, and is open Tuesday through Sunday, 11 a.m. to 2 p.m. (615)388-0462. Reservations are preferred, and the busiest time is during Mule Day, the first weekend in April, and the Majestic Middle Tennessee Home Tour, the two middle weekends in October. MC, V. ($)

MAGNOLIA HOUSE SEAFOOD CASSEROLE

One 5-ounce can shrimp
One 6-ounce can
  crabmeat
1 green pepper, chopped
1 medium onion,
  chopped
1 cup celery, diced

1 cup mayonnaise
1/2 teaspoon salt
Dash Worcestershire
1 cup bread crumbs
Green chili peppers,
  optional

Mix all ingredients. Place in greased casserole and bake 1 hour at 300 degrees. Optional chilies will make a spicier dish.

MAGNOLIA HOUSE CHICKEN DIVAN

Two 10-ounce packages
  frozen broccoli
3 cups cooked, cubed
  chicken
1/4 cup grated sharp
  cheese

1/2 Tablespoon poultry
  seasoning
One 4-ounce can
  mushrooms, drained
  and chopped
1/2 Tablespoon dry
  mustard

One 10 3/4-ounce can
cream of mushroom
soup
One 10 3/4-ounce can
cream of chicken soup

Pepperidge Farm
stuffing mix

Cook broccoli 5 minutes according to package directions. Drain and layer in 8" x 11" Pyrex dish. Cover with cooked chicken. Blend next 6 ingredients and spread over broccoli and chicken. Thickly sprinkle with stuffing mix and bake at 350 degrees until hot and bubbling.

MAGNOLIA HOUSE BROCCOLI CASSEROLE

Two 10-ounce packages
frozen chopped
broccoli, cooked
2 eggs, beaten
One 10 3/4-ounce can
cream of mushroom or
celery soup

1 cup mayonnaise
2 Tablespoons chopped
onion
1 cup sharp cheese,
grated
Crushed Ritz crackers

Combine all ingredients except crackers and blend well. Pour into casserole dish and top with crackers. Bake at 350 degrees about 30 minutes, or until bubbling.

AUNT BEA'S TEA ROOM
Clarksville

When John Donelson's coura-
geous flatboat party made its way down the Holston and Tennessee rivers to the Ohio, and up the Cumberland to Fort Nashborough, they must have marveled at the high banks of the Cumberland at the mouth of the Red River.

Moses Renfroe and his family left Nashville to establish a
station on the bluff in 1780, but were driven off by Indians; the
area was permanently settled four years later.

John Montgomery, a Virginia native of Scotch-Irish descent,
had explored "The West" as a long hunter in 1771, and returned
in 1779 with General George Rogers Clark's Revolutionary
expedition to capture British forts and secure the western
frontier. After the Revolution, Colonel Montgomery was elected
Sheriff at Nashville, and, with surveyor Martin Armstrong,
purchased two hundred acres at the mouth of the Red River.

Named "Clarksville" for General Clark, the second-oldest
town in Middle Tennessee was carefully laid out in 1784. Strict
laws controlled sanitation and behavior in the streets.

On November 11, 1794, Indians attacked Sevier Station at
nearby New Providence, and six people were killed; on November 27, Col. Montgomery and a party of hunters were ambushed
in Western Kentucky, and he was killed while defending a
wounded comrade.

Despite these tragedies and other setbacks, the community on
the bluff continued to prosper. When Tennessee County was
divided in 1796, one of the new counties was named for James
Robertson, and the other for John Montgomery. By 1859, the
population of its county seat had reached five thousand.

At that time, Professor L. D. Ring was conducting a private
school for boys in his house on Fifth Street. His daughter,
Margaret, a music teacher, was the first of several professional
women to live in the house; teacher Martha Edmonson lived
there from 1910 until 1980, when she sold the property to
Bernice and Raybourne Lyle.

The two-story brick house, of vernacular Victorian design, was
evidently remodeled and enlarged in the early twentieth century, when the stairway, formerly in the front hall, was relocated
to an interior room. The Lyles did additional remodeling to

convert it to apartments, but much of this was reversed in 1983, when they adapted it to become a tea room.

Aunt Bea's Tea Room opened in June, 1984, as Clarksville celebrated its bicentennial, and continues to serve delicious weekday lunches in three spacious dining rooms decorated in soft blues.

Popular here are casseroles (ham and broccoli with cheese, beef and noodles, and Chicken Surprise); crisp salads with homemade dressings, and hearty sandwiches; there are also quiches in flaky crusts, soups (try cheese, or meatball) and lovely hot breads. Homemade desserts made by Bernice and her mother, Lottie Parker, might include chocolate cake with chocolate icing, coconut cream cheesecake, or a luscious caramel pie with thick meringue.

Aunt Bea's Tea Room, 111 South Fifth Street, Clarksville, is open Monday through Friday, 11 a.m. to 2 p.m. (615)645-4414. Dress is casual, and reservations are requested for parties of 6 or more. Credit cards are not accepted, although personal checks are. Busiest times are during Oktoberfest and the Montgomery County Fair in September. ($)

AUNT BEA'S BRAN MUFFINS*

1 cup boiling water
1 cup 100% bran cereal
9 Tablespoons
  margarine
2 eggs
1 cup sugar

2 cups buttermilk
2 1/2 cups flour
2 cups All-Bran cereal
2 1/2 teaspoons baking
  soda

In large bowl, pour boiling water over cereal and margarine and stir until margarine is melted. Cool. In mixer bowl, beat eggs and sugar until blended, then beat in buttermilk. Add to cooled bran mixture and beat well. Combine dry ingredients and add to buttermilk mixture just until flour is moistened. Cover bowl tightly and refrigerate at least two hours. Spoon batter into generously greased muffin cups, filling 3/4 full. Bake at 400 degrees until lightly browned and tester comes out clean, about 20 minutes. Serve warm or at room temperature.

AUNT BEA'S CARAMEL PIE*

One 9-inch cooked pie
  crust
3 cups sugar, divided
1/2 cup flour

6 egg yolks (reserve
  whites for meringue)
1/2 teaspoon vanilla
3 cups milk
Dash of salt

In saucepan, mix 2 cups sugar with remaining ingredients and heat to lukewarm, then set aside. In iron skillet, brown one cup sugar to caramel color, stirring constantly. Pour milk mixture into skillet and cook until thickened. Pour into pie crust, cover with meringue and bake at 350 degrees until browned.

For meringue: beat 3 egg whites, a pinch of cream of tartar and a dash of salt until peaks are formed. Add 3 Tablespoons sugar and 1/2 teaspoon vanilla and beat until stiff.

AUNT BEA'S BOILED CUSTARD*

1 cup sugar
2 Tablespoons flour
Pinch of salt

1 quart milk
3 eggs

In saucepan, combine ingredients and cook over low heat until spoon is coated. Cool. Serve with a sprinkle of nutmeg and whipped cream.

* From WELCOME TO AUNT BEA'S TEA ROOM, Bernice Lyle, Clarksville, Tennessee. Used by permission.

TURN OF THE CENTURY
TEA ROOM
Dickson

James Robertson, called "The Father of Middle Tennessee," was born in 1742 in Brunswick County, Virginia, and moved to North Carolina with his family at an early age. When his father died, James, the eldest son, worked to support his family, and did not learn to read until age twenty-six, when he was taught by his wife.

As one of the North Carolina "Regulators," he was a leader of the Wataugans by the time he was thirty. In 1779, his report of rich bottomlands, abundant game, and good water encouraged settlement on the Cumberland River, and in December of that year, he led the overland party to the area that would become Nashville.

Head of the court and colonel of the militia under The Cumberland Compact of 1780, Robertson was named Brigadier General for Middle Tennessee by George Washington in 1790, and was a delegate to Tennessee's constitutional convention in 1796.

Between his duties, Robertson found time to establish the Cumberland Iron Furnace in present-day Dickson County about 1793. The furnace produced some of the cannonballs used during the Battle of New Orleans in 1814.

During the War Between the States, Union troops constructed the Nashville and Northwestern railroad to the Tennessee River. About fourteen miles below Cumberland Furnace, a station was built on the line in 1865; the town which grew up around it was first called "Sneedsville," but was renamed Dickson in 1868.

As a railroad town, Dickson grew rapidly in the post-war years. About 1890, a handsome two-story frame house was built on South Main Street. The Queen Anne-style structure was later altered by the addition of a striking two-story porch and some interior woodwork, but remains a gracious example of its period.

In March, 1983, JoAnn and Harold Sutton opened the Turn of the Century Tea Room on the first floor, then bought the building in 1984 and added on the "Garden Room." This open, airy area with an outdoor feeling is now the main dining room, and three charming Victorian rooms are used for overflow and for private parties.

Tuesday and Thursday luncheon "Tasters Buffet" provides "everything from casseroles to country cooking," JoAnn said.

Thursday night buffets feature a summertime "Salad-a-rama" with fifteen to twenty choices, and do-it-yourself sandwiches and hearty soups in the winter. There's always Steamship Round of Beef on the Sunday buffet.

Menus on other days also reflect the season, and generous portions are the rule. Turkey salad, with a rich old-fashioned flavor, comes with lots of fruit, congealed salad, JoAnn's fragrant muffins, homemade light bread, and southern-style green beans. A good wintertime choice might be seafood quiche, or Gentlemen's Cuisine: Chunks of beef tenderloin in a special sauce, served on rice or noodles with salad and bread.

Weekend dinner entrées prepared to your order include spicy baked Louisiana catfish, charbroiled tenderloin of beef, and mesquite-grilled BJ's Chicken, or you might choose a daily special such as Chicken Baltimore, bursting with crab meat. All come with vegetable, salad, and homemade hot bread.

Desserts range from Miss Anna's yellow loaf cake with burnt-sugar frosting to Hot Fudge Pudding Cake oozing its own sauce and topped with ice cream.

Turn of the Century Tea Room, 303 South Main Street, Dickson, is open for lunch 11 a.m. to 2 p.m., Sunday through Friday, and for dinner 6 to 9 p.m. Thursday through Saturday. (615)446-7300. Dress is casual, reservations are accepted, preferred for dinner, and busiest time is Christmas in the Country arts and crafts festival the first weekend in November. AE, MC, V, Personal Checks. ($$$)

TURN OF THE CENTURY FRENCH MINT TEA

4 cups water
2 Tablespoons dried
  mint
4 tea bags
2 cups water

2 cups orange juice
2 cups pineapple juice
1/2 of 6-ounce can frozen
  lemonade, undiluted

In saucepan, bring mint and 4 cups water to boil. In another saucepan, bring tea bags and 2 cups water to boil and simmer 3 minutes. Strain both, and add juices and undiluted lemonade. Serve over ice; serves about ten.

TURN OF THE CENTURY
MULBERRY GARDEN CASSEROLE

One 6-ounce box Uncle Ben's Long Grain and Wild Rice

One 2-ounce jar pimiento, drained

One 15-ounce can French-style green beans, drained

One 5-ounce can sliced water chestnuts, drained

2 teaspoons finely chopped onion

One 10 3/4-ounce can Campbell's (no substitute) Cream of Celery soup

1 cup Miracle Whip salad dressing

2 cups cooked, diced chicken

Mix all ingredients well, but gently, so as not to break up the beans too much. Bake 30 minutes at 375 degrees.

TURN OF THE CENTURY
MARINATED VEGETABLES

2 cups sugar

2 cups white vinegar

1/3 cup Wesson oil

1/2 teaspoon celery seed

Tomatoes, chopped

Cucumbers, chopped

Onions, chopped

Mix first 4 ingredients and bring just to a boil. Cool, add to vegetables, and allow to sit at least 3 hours. Refrigerate. Any fresh garden vegetables may be used.

JUST A SMALL TOWN
RESTAURANT
Henning

In 1873, Dr. D.M. Henning founded a town in Lauderdale County, about five miles from the county seat of Ripley. It was incorporated in 1883, but dropped its charter, and was re-incorporated in 1901.

When the owner of the local lumber company declared bankruptcy in 1893, ten businessmen co-signed a note so it could be purchased by its manager, a capable Black man named Will Palmer. As he returned the business to prosperity, Palmer also prospered, building a comfortable ten-room bungalow about 1918. From this home, his daughter, Bertha, was married to Simon A. Haley, and here she and their son, Alex, returned in 1921, while Haley completed his education in New York.

Thousands thrilled to the retelling, in his book "Roots" and in the television dramatization, of the stories young Alex first heard on the broad verandah of his grandparents' home. The house was placed on the National Register in 1978.

The Wilson and Company building, constructed in 1886 in Henning's business district, was Henning's only nineteenth-century commercial building saved during a fire one night in 1909. According to tradition, the fire was discovered by a veterinarian returning from a farm visit, who used his gasoline-powered pump to spray the building. The hotel next door was already lost to the flames.

Many buildings were rebuilt that same year; the Wilson Brothers building was for many years a dry goods store called Henning Supply. Recently, it served as a temporary location for the Alex Haley Museum; the building belongs to Mr. Haley.

In October, 1987, returning to his own roots, Henning native John Craig opened a restaurant in half of the first floor, expanding into the former museum. While he was a Houston, Texas, policeman, Craig spent his off-duty hours planning his restaurant and menu. "One of my favorite hobbies was going out to eat," he said. "When I found something I liked, I put it on my menu."

The result is an international cuisine with a distinctly Southern flavor, served in a charming country atmosphere. Candles, flowers, and Victorian wallpaper make it hard to recognize the old drygoods store, and the food and atmosphere belie the name "Just a Small Town Restaurant."

Craig believes in "good service, and a good product at a good price," and ensures it by cutting all his own meats. Prime Rib is popular here, as are broiled fresh Gulf Red Snapper and Tennessee River Catfish. The menu offers a larger-than-usual selection of appetizers and vegetables, all prepared to order.

Desserts include tableside preparations of Bananas Foster and Cherries Jubilee, plus chocolate mousse and homemade chess and lemon icebox pies.

Just a Small Town Restaurant, 110 Main Street, Henning, is open from 11 a.m. to 10 p.m., Monday through Thursday, to 11 p.m. Friday and Saturday, and 11 a.m. to 4 p.m. for the Sunday buffet. A noon buffet is served every day but Saturday. (901)738-2261. Dress is casual, and reservations are accepted, preferred for parties of 6 or more. MC, V. ($$)

JUST A SMALL TOWN VERSION
OF RED SNAPPER HEMINGWAY

**Four 6 to 8-ounce fillets
of red snapper
4 Tablespoons fresh
lemon juice
3 Tablespoons
Worcestershire
Seasoned salt and
freshly ground pepper**

**Flour for dredging
1 egg, beaten
1/4 cup milk
1 cup grated parmesan
cheese
4 Tablespoons olive oil
3 Tablespoons butter
Lemon wedges**

Combine lemon juice and Worcestershire and sprinkle over both sides of fish. Let fish marinate, turning occasionally, 15 minutes. Season fish on both sides, then dredge in flour. In a small bowl, combine egg and milk and beat. Dip fish in egg-milk mixture and then in grated cheese, being sure to coat fish well. In heavy skillet, heat oil and butter until very hot, add fish and sauté about 2 minutes on each side, or until browned. Place skillet in 400 degree oven to finish cooking, about 4 to 5 minutes. Serve immediately with lemon wedges. An excellent variation is to mix a handful of toasted sesame seeds with the grated cheese. Serves 4.

JUST A SMALL TOWN VEGETABLE CASSEROLE

One 20-ounce package
frozen mixed
vegetables OR
One 10-ounce package
frozen peas AND
One 10-ounce package
frozen green beans
1 cup chopped celery

1 cup grated cheddar
cheese
1 cup mayonnaise
1 medium onion,
chopped
1/2 cup margarine,
melted
34 Ritz crackers,
crumbled

In saucepan, cook vegetables and celery until tender, drain, and place in greased casserole. Mix cheese, mayonnaise, and onion well, and place over vegetables. Combine margarine and crackers, and sprinkle over top. Bake 30 minutes at 350 degrees. Serves 6 to 8.

JUST A SMALL TOWN CHOCOLATE MOUSSE

4 ounces semisweet
chocolate
1 Tablespoon brandy

1/2 stick butter
4 eggs, separated
1/3 cup sugar

In double boiler over simmering water, melt chocolate with brandy and butter. Allow to cool about 15 minutes, then add yolks one at the time, beating 2 minutes after each. In large bowl, whip egg whites until they begin to stiffen. Add sugar and whip until they hold firm peaks. Blend chocolate into egg whites gently with a rubber spatula, using lifting motion. Do not stir too much. Refrigerate 6 hours. Serves 4.

FELIX'S RESTAURANT
Germantown

Beautiful Frances Wright, orphaned in 1798 at the age of three, was unusually independent of thought and action. Well educated, and with a substantial inheritance, she and her sister Camilla traveled alone to the United States in 1818. Upon her return to England, Frances wrote a book applauding American life, but opposed to slavery.

Many famous politicians, including Thomas Jefferson, Henry Clay, and the Marquis de Lafayette, praised her writing, and she formed a close friendship with the elderly Lafayette, with whom she toured the United States in 1824-25. At that time she formed a plan for gradual abolition, without loss to slave owners.

Approved by former Presidents Jefferson, Madison, and Monroe, and aided by Andrew Jackson, Frances Wright journeyed to Memphis in 1825 and purchased land on the Wolf River on which to found her colony, Nashoba, in 1826. There, purchased or donated slaves would work out their purchase price while being trained for independence. After training, they would be freed and re-colonized out of the country.

Illness, insufficient money, and ignorance of human nature doomed Nashoba from the beginning, and while Frances was away raising funds, the colony was beset by scandal. In January, 1830, Nashoba ended when its thirty-one Blacks were transported to Haiti.

A nearby settlement, established about the same time as Nashoba, attracted many German immigrants, and was called "Germantown," except during World War I, when the old name of "Nashoba" was used due to anti-German sentiment. Here, about 1928, a one-story commercial building was built by Louis Rosengarten, and used as a variety and dry goods store; its adjacent twin to the north, a grocery and gas station, was built by Stanley Bruce Law.

In what was the center of town near the depot, the little buildings were gathering places for year, but as Germantown grew and shopping patterns changed, they fell into disuse. One side served briefly as a real estate office, but both were empty and abandoned when David Halle purchased them in 1982. He opened the wall between the buildings , and opened a restaurant called "Felix's" in 1983.

With its exposed brick, cypress barn board trim, and bright red benches, Felix's is light and open in the daytime, and cozy at night. Its regular clientele visits three or four times a week, enjoying the menu of American foods they have helped to develop—popular chalkboard items eventually go on the menu.

The result is a wide variety of appetizers that range from baked brie to jalapeño peppers stuffed with cheese; soups and chili, including a great seafood gumbo; hearty sandwiches; and satisfying entrées such as New York Strip and Chicken Parmesan. Everything is fresh, tasty, and attractively presented.

Little children, elderly ladies, and golfers straight from the course all relax at Felix's, finishing off their meals with lemon meringue pie, or deadly Triple Chocolate Brownie: chocolate brownie, chocolate chips, and chocolate cream cheese icing, served hot with melting ice cream.

Felix's, 2285 Germantown Road, South, Germantown, is open from 11 a.m. to 1:30 a.m. daily, with continuous service. Sunday Brunch is served 11 a.m to 3 p.m. (901) 755-6717. All beverages are served, dress is casual, and reservations are not accepted. AE, CB, DC, MC, V, Discover. ($$)

FELIX'S CHICKEN AND HAM SANDWICH WITH HONEY MUSTARD SAUCE

For each serving:

One 3-ounce boned chicken breast	**Hamburger bun, toasted**
	Tomato slice
One 2-ounce slice ham, grilled	**Onion slice**
	Pickle spear
1-ounce slice Swiss cheese	**Parsley for garnish**
	Honey Mustard Sauce (below)

Charbroil chicken breast, then place ham on top, top with cheese and grill until cheese is melted. Place on bun, with tomato, onion, and pickle. Garnish with parsley; serve Honey Mustard sauce on side.

For Honey Mustard Sauce: blend 4 ounces mayonnaise, 1 ounce pure clover honey, and 1/2 ounce Dijon mustard until mixture is the consistency of honey. Chill before serving. Yields enough for 3 sandwiches.

FELIX'S BARTENDER'S NACHOS

For each portion:

6 ounces nacho chips	**1/4 tomato, diced small**
5 ounces grated cheese, divided	**1 Tablespoon diced green onions**
4 ounces chili*	**1 ounce purchased Picante Sauce**
1 cup shredded lettuce	**1 ounce sour cream**

On large ovenproof plate, place chips, top with 1/2 of cheese, then chili, then remaining cheese. Bake at 350 degrees until cheese is melted and chili is hot. Top with lettuce, tomato, and onions, and serve with Picante Sauce and sour cream on the side.

*A thick, meaty homemade chili is suggested.

THE PEABODY HOTEL
Memphis

$\mathbf{T}$he high bluff overlooking the Mississippi River was the site of an Indian village when Hernando De Soto came through in 1541; French and Spanish forts later occupied the area, which remained under Spanish control until the Louisiana Purchase was ratified in 1803.

No permanent European settlement was made until 1819, when, following a treaty with the Chickasaw, John Overton, Andrew Jackson, and James Winchester laid out the town of Memphis.

Memphis grew rapidly; incorporated in 1826, by 1860 it had a population of 33,000 people and was the largest inland cotton market in the world.

One who believed in it was Colonel R.C. Brinkley, who built a seventy-five room hotel on Main Street, at the northwest corner of Monroe, in 1869. Named for philanthropist George Peabody, the hotel was the social center of Memphis for more than fifty years. In 1923, it closed, and a new Peabody Hotel opened in 1925.

The Italian Renaissance Revival structure, filling a city block and rising twelve stories, had five entrances opening into a two-story lobby, dominated by a white marble fountain. Here the famous Peabody Ducks, left in the fountain as a joke, became a time-honored tradition. Guest rooms were the height of luxury, and the Skyway night club, opened in 1939, hosted big-band greats that were broadcast nationally.

Until the mid-1970s, The Peabody was the focus of business and social activity in the mid-South, but several fires, changes in ownership, and the decline of downtown Memphis forced it to close. It was placed on the National Register in 1977.

After a $25 million renovation by the Belz Family of Memphis, The Peabody reopened in 1981, retaining the spirit and appearance of the past, but incorporating modern equipment and standards.

And yes, the Peabody Ducks are back, in person and motif: Dux, an American grill, and Mallards, a dignified lounge, are named for them. Chez Philippe presents extraordinary French cuisine in elegant surroundings, a sumptuous Sunday Brunch is served in the beautifully restored Skyway, and Café Expresso is a deli featuring astounding European-style pastries. You won't go hungry at The Peabody, and, between meals, you can have a drink in the lobby and watch the Ducks— and everyone else in the Western Hemisphere.

The Peabody Hotel, 149 Union Avenue, Memphis, has 452 overnight rooms and 24 suites. (901)529-4000. Breakfast is available at Dux or Café Expresso, which also serve lunch and dinner; Lunch buffet is available at Mallards. Chez Philippe is open for dinner only, 6 to 10 p.m., Monday through Saturday. Sunday Brunch Buffet is 11 a.m. to 2 p.m. in the Skyway. In all restaurants, all beverages are served, and dress is "fashionably casual" in all but Chez Philippe, where coats are required for men. Reservations are recommended. Busiest times are the month of May, during the Great River Carnival in June, and during Oktoberfest in mid October. AE, DC, MC, V, Discover. Chez Philippe ($$$); Dux ($$$); Mallards ($$) Cafe Expresso ($).

DUX MESQUITE-GRILLED CATFISH FILET WITH PAPAYA, RED ONION AND TOMATO VINAIGRETTE

1 papaya, peeled, seeded, diced
1 medium red onion, peeled and diced
2 medium tomatoes, peeled, seeded, diced
1 cup olive oil
Juice of 6 limes
Salt and pepper
Four 8-ounce catfish filets
1/4 cup olive oil

In large bowl, combine papaya with vegetables and oil, and stir in lime juice and seasonings. Prepare charcoal grill with mesquite; when coals are hot, lightly oil and salt and pepper catfish. Grill on each side for about 2 minutes, or until white and firm. Serve immediately with vinaigrette on each filet or on the side. Serves 4.

CHEZ PHILIPPE CATFISH FILET WITH CHAMPAGNE SAUCE AND VEGETABLE CAVIAR

For each serving:
Two 4-ounce filets of catfish
Vegetable Caviar (below)

Salt and pepper
1 ounce fresh salmon
1/4 cup cream
1 egg white

Champagne Sauce
  (below)
Fresh dill for garnish

Cut each filet in three equal parts, lengthwise. Keep the four most attractive and flatten them. In food processor, mix remainder of fish with salmon, seasonings, and egg white. Blend, quickly, add cream, and stop processor immediately; mousse is ready. Spread mousse on two filets; cover with remaining filets. Bake in buttered dish 10 minutes at 450 degrees. Place filets on hot plate, cover with sauce, and garnish with dill.

For Vegetable caviar, cut 1/2 carrot, 1/2 zucchini, and 1/2 turnip into small balls and poach in boiling water.

For Champagne Sauce, reduce 1/2 cup dry champagne by half, with a bit of chopped shallot and 1/2 teaspoon tomato paste. Add 1/3 cup cream, let reduce by 3/5, press through thin strainer, and add vegetable balls.

PEABODY CHEESECAKE

6 ounces graham
  cracker crumbs
1 ounce sugar
1 1/2 ounces unsalted
  butter, melted
1 pound, 4 ounces cream
  cheese

6 ounces sugar
3 eggs
5 1/2 ounces sour cream
1 1/4 ounces whipping
  cream
2 3/4 ounces milk
Dash of vanilla

Mix crumbs and sugar well and stir in melted butter. Press mixture on bottom of greased 9" pan. In mixing bowl, blend cream cheese and sugar until smooth, then add eggs, beating after each, until mixture is fluffy. Add remaining ingredients and stir until combined. Pour mixture in crumb crust and bake in a water bath at 330 degrees for about 1 hour 15 minutes.

RINALDO GRISANTI AND SONS
Memphis

Beale Street, laid out in the 1840s, ran from the Mississippi river to a handsome residential section. Between were an open-air market, where farmers brought their wares, and businesses that catered to farmers.

Tailors, druggists, doctors, and dentists lined the street, but as the neighborhood changed, many were replaced by pawn shops, liquor stores, and saloons with private gambling rooms.

Memphis' first Black band was formed in the late 1860s, and W.C. Handy came to Beale Street in 1908 to lead Thornton's Knights of Pythias Band. Hired by mayoral candidate E.H. Crump, Handy composed the campaign tune later named "Memphis Blues." He also wrote "Beale Street Blues," and "St. Louis Blues."

The Blues was a new art form, an outgrowth of music played by rural Blacks; its popularity made Beale Street a wide-open center of Memphis nightlife, with dance halls, saloons, and theatres (and less respectable places) that never closed.

The Depression and cleanup campaigns shut down some of Beale Street's activities, but there was still music on street corners and in clubs. B.B. King got his start here in the late 1940s, and ten years later, Elvis Presley bought his first suit at Lansky's.

During Urban Renewal, many area buildings were bulldozed, but the Beale Street Historic District was placed on the National Register in 1966, and renovation of some buildings began in the late 1970s. Today, you can still shop at Lansky's or Schwab's Dry Goods, open since 1876. You can still hear The Blues, and you can enjoy a fine Italian meal at Rinaldo Grisanti and Sons.

Chef/owner Ronnie Grisanti is carrying on a tradition begun in 1909, when his grandfather came from Lucca, Italy, and opened a restaurant in downtown Memphis. Success prompted a move to the suburbs, and sons and grandsons opened their own restaurants; there are now five Grisanti restaurants in Memphis.

Ronnie elected to move back downtown in 1985, to two buildings, ca. 1894 and 1919, that have housed, among other things, pawn shops and loan offices. "The city has given us so much," he said. "We're obligated, and this is an opportunity to be part of rebuilding downtown."

His menu reflects his family: Miss Mary's Salad is his grandmother's recipe, dishes are named for relatives, and the house specialty, Pasta ala Elfo, is his father's famous creation.

All dishes are prepared to order; butter rolls, liqueur-soaked cobblers, bread pudding, and fried pies are homemade; vegetables—eight every day for lunch— are Southern; and many pastas, including ravioli, are "handmade." A lot of love and care goes into the food at Rinaldo Grisanti and Sons, and the result is the marvelous food an Italian grandmother would serve her family— if she lived in Memphis.

Rinaldo Grisanti and Sons, 162 Beale Street, Memphis, is open for lunch 11 a.m. to 2:30 p.m., Monday through Friday, and for dinner 5:30 until about 11 p.m., Tuesday through Saturday. (901)527-7668. Dress is casual, all beverages and Italian wines are served, and reservations are accepted for parties of eight or more. Busiest times? "There's something going on all the time," Ronnie Grisanti said. MC, V. ($$)

RINALDO'S SALAD DRESSING

6 ounces pure olive oil
3 ounces red wine
  vinegar
1 1/2 ounces red wine
1/2 ounce crushed black
  pepper

Juice of 1 lemon
1/2 small onion, grated
6 garlic cloves, chopped
1/4 teaspoon salt

In screw-top quart jar, combine all ingredients and mix well. Keeps well at room temperature.

RINALDO GRISANTI AND SONS
PASTA ALA ELFO

8 ounces spaghetti,
  cooked al dente
2 sticks butter
10 cloves garlic, minced
8 jumbo shrimp, raw

1 cup sliced mushrooms
Salt and pepper
6 tablespoons grated
  parmesan cheese
6 ounces white wine*

In large skillet, heat butter and add garlic. Cut shrimp into 3 pieces each; add to skillet. Add mushrooms and cook slowly for 10 minutes over low heat. Add drained spaghetti, Season, add cheese, and cook until spaghetti is very hot. Do not let butter brown. Place on warm serving dish and top with grated cheese. Serves 5. Drink 6 ounces white wine.*

RINALDO GRISANTI AND SONS
SALSÌCCIE ALLA LUCCA

1/2 pound salsìccie
(Italian pork sausage)
1 ounce olive oil
3 ounces white wine,
divided*
1 potato, peeled and
thinly sliced
1 onion, thinly sliced

1/2 cup sliced
mushrooms
2 cups cream sauce
(below)
8 slices mozzarella
cheese
1 cup grated parmesan

In skillet, sauté salsìccie well. Drain, crumble and set aside. Lightly grease casserole dish with olive oil. Pour 1 ounce wine in bottom of dish; drink the other two ounces.* Place potatoes in casserole, top with onions, then salsìccie, then mushrooms. Pour cream sauce over all, top with cheese slices, then sprinkle grated cheese over casserole. Bake 30 minutes at 350 degrees. Serves 4.

For cream sauce: Mix 1 stick butter, melted, 1 pint heavy cream, 1 Tablespoon cornstarch, and 4 ounces grated Swiss cheese in saucepan over low heat. Stir until thick; season with salt and pepper.

*Ronnie Grisanti's instructions.

JUSTINE'S
Memphis

Steamboats from Memphis to New Orleans began regularly scheduled trips in 1826, and commerce between the two cities flourished. Memphians of substance copied New Orleans fashions, competing to build homes that demonstrated their owners' prosperity.

The first residential "subdivision" in Memphis was the division of Dr. Nathaniel Ragland's plantation on Pigeon Roost Road (now Lamar Avenue) into smaller properties. A three acre plot, bordered by the Memphis and Charleston Railroad, was purchased in 1843 by Nathaniel and Mildred Anderson, who had come to Memphis from Virginia in 1823. Anderson was a cotton broker and banker who divided his time between concerns in Memphis and New Orleans.

Their impressive Italianate house on Pigeon Roost Road was probably built when their first home burned in 1850. An L-shaped, two-story structure, the facade of the brick house was covered in pink stucco. It was sold about 1856 to H.M. Grosvenor, a Massachusetts native in the furniture business.

Following the War Between the States, Grosvenor mortgaged his home to William D. Coward, who took over the property in 1867 upon Grosvenor's death, and deeded it to his son, Samuel Coward. It remained in the family until it was sold in 1957 to become a restaurant. As the Anderson-Coward house, it was placed on the National Register in 1986.

Embellished and enlarged over the years, the house was returned to the feeling of its original period by Justine and Dayton Smith. A porch was removed, front windows were matched to the remaining original, and missing details were hand crafted or supplied from buildings of the period; the wrought-iron stair rail came from the old Gayoso Hotel.

The beautiful old house, elegantly redecorated, made a perfect new home for Justine's restaurant, a successful operation begun in downtown Memphis in 1948. Without fanfare, Justine's French cuisine had achieved national recognition in just a few years, and when the lease on her original building ran out, it was time to expand.

Justine's has been one of Memphis' favorite places for forty years, and still serves the same classic French food, with the same courteous, old-fashioned service, that patrons from all over the country have come to expect.

Popular here are the lengthy list of appetizers, including justly-famous Crab Meat Justine, and Oysters Justine (with artichoke hearts); steaks (meat cut on the premises); and fresh seafood. A casserole of shrimp, crab, and mushrooms, and curries of chicken, shrimp, or crab are distinctive, and desserts consist of classic favorites (Baked Alaska, Cherries Jubilee, etc.) plus homemade Lotus ice cream, Rum Cream Pie, and a crisp, crunchy Macaroon Pie topped with ice cream.

Justine's, 919 Coward Place, Memphis, is at the end of East Street, six blocks south of Union Avenue, and offers valet parking in a secured lot. It is open for dinner only, Monday through Saturday, 5:30 p.m. to 12 Midnight. (901)527-9973. All beverages and an extensive wine list are available, coat and tie are required for men, and reservations are requested, required for parties of ten or more and during the month of December. AE, DC, MC, V. ($$$)

CRAB MEAT JUSTINE

1/4 pound butter
1 cup dry sherry
1/2 pound fresh lump
　　crab meat
Dash of Worcestershire

Dash of Tabasco
Squeeze of lemon
Sliced French bread,
　　toasted
Hollandaise sauce*

In skillet, melt butter, and add all ingredients in order listed, taking care not to boil or burn mixture. Place about 2 Tablespoons of mixture on a slice of toasted French bread, and top with Hollandaise sauce. Lightly brown in a very hot oven.

*Most general cookbooks have a recipe for this classic sauce.

JUSTINE'S STUFFED MUSHROOMS

24 large mushrooms,
　　cleaned
3 ounces butter

1 teaspoon flour
5 ounces heavy cream
Salt and white pepper

1 ounce shallots,
chopped
5 ounces white wine
2 teaspoons parsley,
chopped
6 ounces flaked crab
meat

Tabasco
Bread crumbs
Dash of paprika
4 Tablespoons white
wine
1/2 stick melted butter

Remove mushroom stems, chop finely, and reserve. Sauté caps and shallots in butter until shallots are golden brown. Add wine; cover and simmer 1 minute. Remove caps. Add chopped stems and parsley to wine sauce. Simmer uncovered about 1/2 minute. Add crab meat and sprinkle with flour; stir while adding cream. Simmer until mixture thickens. Season, and stuff caps with mixture. Place caps in buttered baking dish, sprinkle with bread crumbs and paprika, then wine and melted butter. Bake in very hot oven just until browned. Serves 4.

JUSTINE'S RUM CREAM PIE

2 cups crushed graham
crackers
1/2 pound butter,
softened
1 1/2 cups sugar, divided
2 cups whipping cream
7 egg yolks, beaten to
lemon color

1/2 cup rum
2 Tablespoons
unflavored gelatin,
dissolved
2 squares unsweetened
chocolate, grated, for
garnish

Mix 1/2 cup sugar with butter and crumbs and press into two 9-inch pie pans. Bake in medium oven a few minutes; remove and chill. Whip cream and set aside. Mix remaining ingredients, fold in cream, and pour half of the mixture into each crust. Top with sprinkling of grated chocolate. Serve chilled. Yields 2 pies.

LA TOURELLE
Memphis

Memphis was incorporated in 1826, when it encompassed less than a square mile, and had a population under 500. As it grew in size and reputation, people from Tennessee and the surrounding states were attracted, then investors from New England and immigrants from Ireland and Germany.

Often rough in the early days, it soon settled into an industrious business community connected by steamboat with New Orleans and Cincinnati. The Memphis and Charleston Railroad, completed in 1857, gave access to the Atlantic seaboard, and increased the town's usefulness as a distribution center.

Memphis was under Confederate control early in the War Between the States, but following a ninety-minute river battle in June, 1862, Union troops took over for the remainder of the war.

Readjustment was difficult; Memphis was overflowing with camp followers, jobless freed slaves, and criminals. Outbreaks of yellow fever decimated the population, as thousands fled the city and many of those remaining died. Without fully understanding the cause of yellow fever, medical authorities improved sanitary conditions, and helped to wipe out the disease.

By 1890, Memphis was growing again, with a population of nearly 65,000, and the city limits were extended to twelve square miles in 1898. The opening of Overton Park encouraged development in the northeastern part of the city, and on an extension of Monroe Street, a quaint brick cottage in the Queen Anne style was built with a corner tower.

The tower led to its name, "La Tourelle," when the little house became a French restaurant in 1977. Decorated in warm peach with white trim, and showcasing works by local artists, it is owned by Memphis State University Track Coach Glenn Hayes and his wife Martha, a French teacher.

Glenn did all the cooking the first summer, with Martha baking the breads; they utilized a set menu that changed weekly. After five years, they went to a menu with both a la carte and prix fixe listings, an unusual step that provides excellent value.

La Tourelle follows the classic French repertoire, with traditional dishes creatively prepared. Fresh fish is hand cut, fresh herbs are ordered from Mississippi, and all sauces and reductions are made on the premises, with plenty of cream and butter.

Dinner here might begin with Leek and Chervil Soup; continue with Smoked Salmon with Shallots and Green Peppercorns, or green salad with walnuts; and go on to Duck with Raspberry Vinegar, or Swordfish with Mustard Butter.

La Tourelle's most popular dessert is chocolate-almond Queen Mother Cake, an Australian delicacy, but there are always homemade ice creams and other tempting choices, such as Baked Gratin of Raspberries with Crème Anglaise.

La Tourelle, 2146 Monroe, Memphis, is just off Cooper Street, one block north of Union Avenue. It is open for dinner only, Monday through Saturday, from 6 p.m. Last seating is 9:30. (901)726-5771. All beverages are available, most men wear coats and ties, and reservations are advisable. La Tourelle is closed the week after New Year's and the first week in September. MC, V. ($$$)

LA TOURELLE
TUNA MARINATED IN TARRAGON

20 ounces tuna
2 ounces olive oil
2 bunches fresh
   tarragon, divided
1 onion, minced
1 Tablespoon unsalted
   butter
1 teaspoon sugar

1/2 10-ounce box frozen
   green peas
1 Tablespoon onion,
   chopped
1/3 cup white wine
1 ounce heavy cream
1 pound butter, softened
Salt and pepper

Cut tuna into 1 1/2-ounce medallions and marinate 24 hours in oil and 1 bunch tarragon. In saucepan, mix onion, butter, and 1/2 bunch tarragon, chopped, with sugar and water to cover. Cook on low heat for 20 to 30 minutes and reserve. In blender, purée peas with a little water and remaining tarragon. Set aside. In saucepan, mix onion with wine and reduce until almost dry. Add cream, then lower heat to medium and whisk in butter, piece by piece. DO NOT BOIL! Add purée of peas and set in warm spot for 20 minutes; put through sieve and season. Grill or sauté tuna to medium rare (or desired doneness), divide onion mixture onto 4 plates, divide tuna medallions on top, and coat with sauce. Serves 4.

LA TOURELLE QUEEN MOTHER CAKE

6 ounces semi-sweet
  chocolate
1 1/2 sticks unsalted
  butter
2/3 cup sugar

6 eggs, separated
1 1/4 cups finely ground
  almonds
Icing (below)

Melt chocolate over simmering water; set aside. In large bowl, cream butter, add sugar and blend well, then beat in egg yolks. Add slightly cooled chocolate, then almonds. In another large bowl, beat egg whites to soft peaks, and fold carefully into chocolate mixture. Line bottom of 8" pan with waxed paper, butter paper, and pour in mixture. Bake about 30 minutes at 350 degrees; cake should be moist. Spread cooled icing on cooled cake.

For icing: Melt 8 ounces semi-sweet chocolate with 1/2 cup heavy cream; stir until smooth, then cool slightly.

LA TOURELLE CASSIS ICE CREAM

8 cups half and half
  cream
1 cup sugar
1 1/2 Tablespoons vanilla

1 1/2 cups cassis (or
  other black currant
  liqueur)
One 18-ounce jar
  seedless blackberry
  jam

Mix all ingredients together, pour into ice cream maker, and freeze according to manufacturer's directions.

CAFÉ SOCIETY
Memphis

In 1900, Memphis' first Board of Park Commissioners was formed. Their "City Beautiful" program established 335 acres on the city's northwest boundary as Overton Park, and the scenic parkway system which encircled the city.

With the expansion of trolley routes into the suburbs and the beginning of automobile traffic, more streets were paved, and planned residential neighborhoods boomed. Between 1900 and the mid 1920s, numerous subdivisions were developed.

In the Evergreen Historic District, placed on the National Register in 1985, attractive and well-maintained houses remain as fine examples of the architectural styles popular during the period.

One of the few commercial structures in the district is a one-story brick veneer business row with a flat roof, built near the corner of Poplar Avenue about 1920. Many offices and shops were housed there over the years, but by the late 1970s it had deteriorated into used-appliance stores.

Michel Leny (pronounced Lenny) son of a Belgian chef who worked at Maxim's in Paris, came to Memphis in 1966. Encouraged to become a hairdresser despite culinary leanings, he operated his own salon, but yearned for a restaurant.

The two end shops in the Evergreen row were his answer. "It was a shell," Michel said. "I did all the design here." The result is an open space with a European cafe atmosphere, called "Café Society" after a restaurant in Paris. Bright and airy at lunchtime, it becomes romantically dim in the evenings, with candles and flowers on the small tables.

The casual, pleasant feeling is fostered by the staff, many of whom were present on opening day in May, 1987. "Everybody feels very much a part of it," said Manager/Partner Bill Tomlinson, "and everybody takes a lot of pride. We're really quality conscious."

Food here is International, emphasizing Belgian home cooking (Belgian Stew: beef tenderloin cooked in beer with onions and mushrooms), French favorites (Coq au Vin), and some inventions of Michel and his father (Sole Maurice, with crab meat and creamed spinach).

There are wonderful soups served in hard rolls, interesting appetizers, and at lunch, salads and sandwiches. Sunday Brunch provides Belgian waffles, traditional egg dishes, and poached quail.

Popular desserts include Belgian Chocolate Mousse, Brandy Alexanders made with ice cream, and Chocolate Ice Cream Puff, a fat cream puff filled with French vanilla ice cream, and topped with Belgian chocolate sauce.

CaféSociety, 212 North Evergreen, Memphis, is open for lunch 11:30 a.m. to 2 p.m. Tuesday through Friday, for dinner 5 to 10 p.m. Tuesday through Thursday, to 11 p.m. Friday and Saturday. Sunday Brunch is 11:30 a.m. to 2 p.m. (901)722-2177. All beverages are served, with many wines available by the glass, dress is casual, and reservations are not accepted; parties are seated in order of arrival. AE, MC, V. ($$)

CAFÉ SOCIETY OYSTERS MAURICE

1/2 pound chopped raw shrimp
6 Tablespoons butter, divided
2 dozen oysters
1/2 to 1 cup milk
2 Tablespoons white wine

3 Tablespoons flour
1 egg yolk, beaten
1/4 teaspoon white pepper
1 teaspoon salt
1/4 cup bread crumbs
1/4 cup grated gruyere cheese

In skillet, melt 2 Tablespoons butter, add shrimp, and cook 2 to 3 minutes. Set aside. Pour oyster liquor in measuring cup and add milk to make 1 3/4 cups. Stir in wine. In heavy skillet, melt remaining butter, stir in flour, and whisk. Cook over high heat until boiling and slightly thickened. Reduce heat and simmer 3 minutes. Blend 1/4 cup sauce with beaten egg yolk, then add mixture to skillet. Add seasoning, remove from heat, and stir in shrimp.

Fill baking dish with rock salt and place oyster shells on it. In each shell, spoon one Tablespoon of shrimp sauce, top with oyster and additional spoon of sauce. Sprinkle with bread

212

crumbs and cheese. Broil, 3 inches from flame, 1 or 2 minutes, or until brown. Serves 4.

CAFÉ SOCIETY RED CABBAGE

4 Tablespoons butter
2 cups white onion,
  sliced
8 cups red cabbage,
  shredded

1/2 cup white vinegar
2 apples, sliced
1 cup brown sugar
Salt and pepper

In large skillet, melt butter, cook onions about 10 minutes, or until soft. Add cabbage and mix, then add vinegar, apples, and sugar and cook about 15 minutes. Stir well and cook 1 hour 15 minutes. Salt and pepper to taste.

CAFÉ SOCIETY MUSHROOM SKILLET

4 Tablespoons chopped
  shallots
2 Tablespoons butter
3/4 pound mushrooms,
  finely chopped
1 cup Bechamel sauce*
1 teaspoon chopped
  parsley
Salt and pepper

Twenty-four 2-inch
  mushroom caps
2 Tablespoons bread
  crumbs
1 Tablespoon grated
  cheese
2 Tablespoons butter, in
  tiny pieces

In heavy skillet, cook shallots in butter until soft. Add chopped mushrooms and cook 10 minutes. Transfer to large bowl, stir in Bechamel and parsley and season to taste. Fill mushroom caps. Mix crumbs and cheese and sprinkle over the filling. Butter a large shallow baking dish and place filled caps in it; dot with butter and bake for 10 or 15 minutes at 400 degrees. Serves 6.
  *Most general cookbooks have a recipe for this classic sauce.

INDEX TO RESTAURANTS

INDEX TO RECIPES

Ham Hocks and Black-eyed
Peas, The Donoho Hotel, 113
Lamb Chops Lynchburg, The
Radisson Read House, 89
Marinated Pork Chops,
Manhattan's, 76
Sausìccie alla Lucca, Rinaldo
Grisanti and Sons, 201
Veal Imperial, Peoples of
Carter's Court, 168
Veal Oskar, Hale Springs
Inn, 44

POULTRY

Apple Walnut Chicken,
Hawkeye's Corner, Too, 80
Basil Chicken Rotini, Mere
Bulles, 134
Boneless Breast of Chicken
Romano, Union Station
Hotel, 148
Bungalow Chicken, The Bunga-
low, 93
Cheezy Baked Breast of
Chicken, Tennessee Walking
Horse Hotel, 132
Chicken and Ham Sandwich,
Felix's Restaurant, 192
Chicken Divan, Magnolia
House, 176
Chicken Enchiladas,
Manhattan's, 77
Chicken Salad, Ruby
Tuesday, 69
Chicken Stir Fry, Kingsport
Grocery Co., 36
Cranberry Chicken, Peoples of
Carter's Court, 168
Duck Grand Marnier, The
Courtyard Café, 84
Hot Chicken Casserole, The
Stuffed Goose, 124

Mulberry Garden Casserole,
Turn of the Century, 185
Rachel's Creamed Chicken,
Peoples of Carter's Court, 169
Southern Fried Chicken, The
Donoho Hotel, 112
Spicy Chicken Gumbo, The
Bistro at the Bijou, 60
Triple Decker Chicken Salad
Sandwich, The Attic Restau-
rant, 48
Uncle Harry's Smoked Turkey
Salad, Firehouse
Restaurant, 25

SALADS AND DRESSINGS

Apricot Salad, The Stuffed
Goose, 125
Blue Cheese Dressing, Stock
Yard Restaurant, 156
Chicken Salad, Ruby
Tuesday, 69
Churchill's House Salad and
Dressing, Churchill's, 96
Cranberry Waldorf Congealed
Salad, Choices
Restaurant, 172
Doak House Salad Dressing,
The Doak House, 41
Dressing for Spinach Salad,
Perry's, 100
Frozen Fruit Salad, The Corner
House, 117
Luncheon Shrimp Salad, The
Corner House, 116
Oriental Salad, The Courtyard
Café, 84
Raspberry Vinaigrette Dressing,
Mère Bulles, 136
Rinaldo's Salad Dressing, Ri-
naldo Grisanti and Sons, 200
Roasted Red Pepper Vinaigrette,
Chefs on Command, 152

Sweet and Sour Salad Dressing,
Blue Iris Tearoom, 29
Thousand Island Dressing,
Wonderland Hotel, 52
Uncle Harry's Smoked Turkey
Salad, Firehouse
Restaurant, 25

SANDWICHES

Chicken and Ham Sandwich,
Felix's Restaurant, 192
Philly Steak Sandwich,
Manhattan's, 77
Triple Decker Chicken Salad
Sandwich, The Attic Restaurant, 48

SAUCES

Tennessee Barbecue Sauce, Miss
Mary Bobo's Boarding
House, 129

SEAFOODS AND FRESH WATER FISH

Baked Stuffed Filet of Flounder,
Union Station Hotel, 148
Blackened Catfish, Jimmy
Kelly's, 160
Ceviche, Troutdale Dining
Room, 16
Chez Philippe Catfish Filet with
Champagne Sauce and Vegetable Caviar, The Peabody
Hotel, 196
Crab Cakes, The Merchants, 140
Crab meat Dressing for Stuffed
Trout, The Doak House, 41
Crab meat Justine,
Justine's, 204
Dux Mesquite-Grilled Catfish
Filet with Papaya, Red Onion,
and Tomato Vinaigrette, The
Peabody Hotel, 196

Lobster Bisque a la Hermitage,
The Hermitage Hotel, 144
Lobster Sauté, Chefs on Command, 152
Luncheon Shrimp Salad, The
Corner House, 116
Marinade for Tuna Steak with
Soy and Ginger, Perry's, 101
New England Clam Chowder,
L & N Seafood Grill, 68
Oysters Florentine, Perry's, 100
Oysters Maurice, Café
Society, 212
Red Snapper Hemingway, Just a
Small Town Restaurant, 188
Red Snapper with Ginger,
Churchill's, 97
Salmon en Croute with Lime
Sauce, The Hermitage
Hotel, 145
Scampi Trieste, Mario's, 164
Seafood Casserole, Magnolia
House, 176
Seafood Jardinaire, Mère
Bulles, 137
Shrimp and Hearts Casserole,
The Bungalow, 92
Shrimp Français, Troutdale
Dining Room, 17
Tuna Marinated in Tarragon, La
Tourelle, 208

SOUPS

Bacon and Cheese Soup,
Hundred Oaks Castle, 120
Belgian Leek Soup, The Soup
Kitchen, 64
Bisque of Squash and Apple,
Churchill's, 97
Cheese and Mushroom Soup,
Kingsport Grocery Co., 36
Cream of Broccoli Soup, The
Doak House, 40

VEGETABLES

DINING IN HISTORIC TENNESSEE
Mail to:
McClanahan Publishing House, Inc.
P.O. Box 100
Kuttawa, Kentucky 42055

Please send me _____ copies of

DINING IN HISTORIC TENNESSEE	**@ $14.00 each**	_____
Postage and Handling	**@ $2.00 each**	_____
Kentucky residents add 5% sales tax	**@ .70 each**	_____
Total		_____

Make check payable to McClanahan Publishing House

Ship To:
Name_____

Address_____

City _____State_____Zip_____

— —

DINING IN HISTORIC TENNESSEE
Mail to:
McClanahan Publishing House, Inc.
P.O. Box 100
Kuttawa, Kentucky 42055

Please send me _____ copies of

DINING IN HISTORIC TENNESSEE	**@ $14.00 each**	_____
Postage and Handling	**@ $2.00 each**	_____
Kentucky residents add 5% sales tax	**@ .70 each**	_____
Total		_____

Make check payable to McClanahan Publishing House

Ship To:
Name_____

Address_____

City _____State_____Zip_____